THEATRE SYMPOSIUM

A PUBLICATION OF THE SOUTHEASTE

In Other Habits: Thea

Volume 26

Published by the

Southeastern Theatre Conference and

The University of Alabama Press

THEATRE SYMPOSIUM is published annually by the Southeastern Theatre Conference, Inc. (SETC), and by the University of Alabama Press. SETC nonstudent members receive the journal as a part of their membership under rules determined by SETC. For information on membership, write to SETC, 1175 Revolution Mill Drive, Studio 14, Greensboro, NC 27405. All other inquiries regarding subscriptions, circulation, purchase of individual copies, and requests to reprint materials should be addressed to the University of Alabama Press, Box 870380, Tuscaloosa, AL 35487-0380.

THEATRE SYMPOSIUM publishes works of scholarship resulting from a single-topic meeting held on a southeastern university campus each spring. A call for papers to be presented at that meeting is widely publicized each autumn for the following spring. Information about the next symposium is available from Sarah McCarroll, Georgia Southern University, Department of Communication Arts, 1332 Southern Drive, Statesboro, GA 30458, smccarroll @ georgiasouthern.edu.

THEATRE SYMPOSIUM
A PUBLICATION OF THE SOUTHEASTERN THEATRE CONFERENCE

Volume 26   *Contents*   **2018**

Introduction   5
  Sarah McCarroll

Plus que Reine: The Napoleonic Revival in Belle Epoque
  Theatre and Fashion   11
  Michele Majer

Creating a Realistic Rendering Pedagogy: The Fashion
  Illustration Problem   40
  Caitlin Quinn

Where'd I Put My Character?: The Costume Character
  Body and Essential Costuming for the Ensemble Actor   49
  Aly Renee Amidei

Embracing the Chaos: Creating Costumes for
  Devised Work   58
  Kyla Kazuschyk

Dressing the Image: Costumes in Printed Theatrical
  Advertising   72
  David S. Thompson

Costuming the Audience: Gentility, Consumption,
  and the Lady's Theatre Hat in Gilded Age America   88
  Leah Lowe

The RuPaul Effect: The Exploration of the Costuming
  Rituals of Drag Culture in Social Media and the
  Theatrical Performativity of the Male Body in the
  Ambit of the Everyday   100
  Jorge Sandoval

A Brand New Day on Broadway: The Genius of Geoffrey
   Holder's Artistry and His Intentional Evocation of the
   African Diaspora   118
      Gregory S. Carr

"On the [Historical] Sublime": J. R. Planché's *King John*
   and the Romantic Ideal of the Past   127
      Andrew Gibb

Contributors   141

Introduction

Sarah McCarroll

IN THE FINAL MOMENTS of Shakespeare's *Twelfth Night*, the Count Orsino says to Viola, newly revealed as a woman,

> . . . Cesario, come—
> For so you shall be while you are a man,
> But when in other habits you are seen,
> Orsino's mistress and his fancy's queen. (5.1.387–90)

The word "habit" here obviously and explicitly refers to garments. Cesario remains Cesario, and a man, while dressed in male garments, but upon assumption of Viola's female clothing, will become a woman who is a suitable love match for the noble Orsino. There is a double meaning in Orsino's turn of phrase, however; habit, of course, also means a pattern of behavior, an ingrained practice, which is repeated to the extent that it becomes routine. What Shakespeare's wordplay calls attention to is the way in which our habits (clothing) influence or even dictate the way we and others understand our habits (tendencies) of behavior. When we dress in a certain manner, we are expected and perhaps expect ourselves to behave in a way that matches our clothing.

When we examine this dynamic of dress from a theatrical perspective, we immediately encounter something that seems almost self-evident, and which costume designers know instinctively and are trained to exploit: the manner in which we costume a character creates audience expectations for that character. The costume provides information to the audience about who the characters are, how they function within the world of the play, and how they might be expected to behave. Costumes also work to provide information to the actor who assumes a character; I've had more than one actor say to me, "I don't know my character until I have my shoes," or some other costume piece deemed essential to getting into the character's skin. There it is: the costume can work as the character's skin—something to be stepped inside, assumed—and putting it on means putting on not just the garments, but the habits of the character.

Perhaps because of their inescapably intimate relationship to the actor's body, perhaps because fragile materials mean that costumes do not necessarily survive from historical productions, perhaps also because the creation processes of costumes are connected to skills traditionally understood as "women's work," like weaving and sewing, theatrical costume has been under-theorized and under-examined historically. Theatrical design fields and production elements in general tend to be dealt with as craft, so that meaning-making is understood as a process whereby designers manipulate elements and principles of design: line, shape and silhouette, color, symmetry and balance; craftspeople then construct pieces for use onstage based on those designs. Important historical productions receive analysis, but it is often focused on just these dynamics of manipulation. Analysis of the ways in which meaning is made via these visual elements often stops at the ways in which designs support and communicate the given circumstances of text or the production's conceptual approach.

This is true across the theatrical design fields, but I often have the sense that it is more true of costume than of other design areas. While there are certainly exceptions (*Shakespeare and Costume*, edited by Patricia Lennox and Bella Mirabella, for example), theatrical costume is most usually written about in a variety of "how-to" texts, which are focused on practice: how to design for the stage, how to construct costumes. To my mind, some of this has to do with the way the word "costume" is used. A quick Google Books search of the term "historic costume" reveals that most books on the subject are actually focused on historic *clothing*, not costume, in the way theatre practitioners understand the term. Even in theatre, we often think of costumes as "the clothes the character wears." This is true, of course, but it serves to deemphasize the larger ways in which theatrical costume is a part of the deeply systemic creation of meaning onstage, a process that would benefit from rigorous analysis at every stage.

At work, too, are the divides in theatrical training, which see designers and technicians routed through one system of heavily practice-focused courses, while historians and theoreticians take what a graduate school peer of mine referred to as "the egghead classes." This separation means that, by and large, theoretical explorations of dress are found in discussions of clothing worn in daily life rather than in analyses of costume for the stage: *The Fashioned Body: Fashion, Dress and Social Theory* (Joanne Entwhistle), *Thinking through Fashion: A Guide to Key Theorists* (edited by Agnès Rocamora), and *Dress History: New Directions in Theory and Practice* (edited by Charlotte Nicklas and Annebella Pollen) to name only a few. The clothing of the past is well examined with survey texts and often lavishly illustrated exhibit catalogues from major museums with costume collections. (Those produced under Harold Koda's leadership of the Metropolitan Museum of Art's Costume Institute include retrospectives of Charles James and Paul Poiret.) But again, the emphasis is on garments worn in daily life, whether that life is courtly or common.

These habits of training and scholarship result in a gap where there might otherwise be more substantive explorations of theatrical costume, and the ways in which theory, history, and practice inform and rely upon one another. Theatre Symposium 26, held on the campus of Agnes Scott College on April 7–8, 2017, saw a diverse group of scholar-artist-practitioners gather to explore what close analyses of stage costume might reveal about how meaning is created onstage, and the underlying assumptions embedded in theatrical practice and costume production.

It has been my experience that one of the great strengths of Theatre Symposium is the way in which it brings together researchers engaged in more traditional historical, theoretical, or archival research with practitioners engaged in creative scholarship. The conversations of the weekend inevitably discover commonalities across the arbitrary divide often imposed between "scholars" and "artists." At Theatre Symposium, it is always clear that practice is scholarship and that historical and archival research are at their best when they are supported by a lively understanding of how a production gets into performance. This dynamic—this habit—of Theatre Symposium is evident in the essays presented here.

The volume begins with history: Michele Majer's keynote address examines the ways in which "reproductions" of First Empire French dress were created and staged in the early years of the twentieth century. The ways that these costumes were constructed and presented call attention to complex relationships among theatre, couture fashion, and methods of manufacture. The circular transmission of ideas and images between historical art, theatrical production, and fashionable style makers speaks clearly to the ways in which theatrical costumes may become deeply embedded in creating larger social habits of dress.

The following three essays are based in each author's professional practice with each one interested in how habits of costume design form systems of meaning onstage and in the production process. Caitlin Quinn's exploration of her students' struggles in rendering realistic, inclusive body types invites consideration of the ways in which systemic inclusion must become a habit at every level and stage of the theatrical process. Aly Renee Amidei examines how the often practically necessitated use of actors in multiple roles in a single production may be turned to advantage if a costumer can facilitate the creation of a "composite body" via the skillful use of iconic garments or costume pieces. The sometime insanity of working in devised theatre provides the occasion for Kyla Kazuschyk's discussion of ways in which a flexible designer can open doors to the creation of timely, topical meanings by providing, often at very short notice, costumes that respond to immediately current world events.

If these three essays are concerned with the habits of theatrical costume production, the next three pieces take up questions of reception and the audience. David S. Thompson surveys the ways in which costumes have been presented in theatre advertising over time, with an eye toward uncovering the ways in which the usage of images of costumed actors might manipulate audience expectation and consumption. Leah Lowe's essay positions the theatre hats of Gilded Age America as their own kind of "theatrical costume," part of social performances based in habits of dress just as constructed as those occurring in front of the footlights. Jorge Sandoval takes another perspective on the word "theatrical" in his essay, scrutinizing the ways in which the theatricalized dress and behavior of drag queens becomes commodified and therefore politically neutralized through comic presentation on the reality TV show *RuPaul's Drag Race*.

The volume returns to archival research, and specific theatrical designs and designers, with Gregory S. Carr's appreciation and exploration of Geoffrey Holder's iconic costume designs for 1975's *The Wiz*, which used costume as a visual journey into the African American experience, the form of the costumes calling attention to the themes of the musical. The volume closes where it began, with more distant theatrical history. J. R. Planché's 1823 designs for Charles Kemble's *King John* are often cited as being the first historically accurate costumes for a major production. Andrew Gibb situates the production in the context of the burgeoning theatrical antiquarian movement of the period but looks further, to the Romantic habits of mind that shaped the costumes' appearance. The pieces in this volume underscore the ways in which the habits that clothe actors onstage are ultimately reflective of the social, intellectual, and theatrical habits of an historical moment.

As so many of the essays here illustrate, producing costumes for the theatre is a necessarily collaborative event, involving a multiplicity of people. The same is absolutely true of planning the physical event of Theatre Symposium, as well as of producing this journal. Keynote speaker Michele Majer, who spends much of her time working in clothing and textile history, graciously agreed to immerse herself in theatre for a weekend; her insights and questions essentially brought an audience member's perspective to the work of the many theatre practitioners who presented, while her address (the first chapter of this volume) provided a model for ways in which costumes, theatrical ephemera, and production history can be braided into larger analyses of the ways in which theatre fits into society. In addition, while it is not possible to include every paper presented during the symposium, every attendee and presenter is due thanks for their contributions to the stimulating conversations of the weekend.

I would like to express my deepest gratitude to the inimitable David S. Thompson, the Annie Louise Harrison Waterman Professor of Theatre at Agnes Scott College, past editor of *Theatre Symposium*, and our host for the April event. His smooth handling of so many logistical details makes preparations for the event worry-free for an editor. Thanks are also due to the administration, faculty, and staff of Agnes Scott for allowing us to utilize their facilities and recharge with walks on their lovely campus. In particular, Leah Owenby, whose good humor and flexibility make day-of arrangements an enjoyment rather than a burden; Megan Simmons, who shows endless patience instructing a Luddite like me in operating video-conferencing programs; and Pete Miller, Director of Dining Services, who along with his marvelous staff sees to it that bodies are as well fed as minds, must be directly acknowledged. Additionally, Theatre Symposium would not be possible either as a meeting or a published journal without the support of SETC. Executive Director Betsey Horth and the central office staff, including Jean Wentz, do much to lighten an editor's load.

I always leave the Theatre Symposium weekend refreshed and intellectually recharged, and it has been a great pleasure to find that the editing process for this volume has only deepened those feelings. It would not be possible to produce this volume without the service of the Theatre Symposium editorial board, whose cogent and thoughtful commentaries help to shape the volume as a whole, as well as individual papers. I am indebted to those past editors of Theatre Symposium who have offered unstinting advice, support, and encouragement: J. K. Curry, Philip G. Hill, Scott Phillips, David S. Thompson, and E. Bert Wallace. In addition, I cannot say enough to thank immediate past editor Becky Becker, who has served as mentor and guide to me not only with regard to Theatre Symposium, but with so much related to the crazy journey that is a career in the academy. Associate editor Andrew Gibb has been an invaluable collaborator in this process; his insightful comments have done much to shape the work here, he seems always to be able to see the forest for the trees as an essay takes shape, and he is a marvel at finding that word that you're looking for but can't quite think of. Dan Waterman, Joanna Jacobs, and Eric Schramm at the University of Alabama Press have an unending store of patience which they graciously share during the editing and proofreading process.

I would be remiss if I did not thank the administration at Georgia Southern University, especially Dr. Pamela Bourland-Davis, Chair of the Department of Communication Arts, and Dr. Curtis Ricker, Dean of the College of Liberal Arts and Social Sciences. In a world of ever-tighter academic budgets, they found a way to offer me course release time, making it possible for me to accept this term as editor while maintaining my responsibilities in the classroom and as resident designer and costume shop manager for the Theatre and Performance Program. My colleagues in Theatre, Lisa Abbott, Kelly Berry, Nicholas Newell, and Katie Rasor, also offer unwavering support that allows me to practice both traditional research and creative scholarship simultaneously. Finally, personal thanks are due to my mother, Dr. Roberta Rankin, who somehow manages to know when I want her advice as a theatre professional and when I just want to talk to Mom; she is my mainstay.

Plus que Reine

The Napoleonic Revival in Belle Epoque Theatre and Fashion

Michele Majer

IN 1899, THE CENTENARY of the coup d'état that created the Consulate and brought him closer to the imperial throne, Napoleon Bonaparte was, as one writer put it, "à la mode."[1] Although the cult of Napoleon was established while the emperor was still alive and it remained strong throughout the nineteenth century, as Venita Datta discusses in *Heroes and Legends of Fin-de-Siècle France: Gender, Politics, and National Identity*, it enjoyed renewed interest between 1890 and 1914, a period during which the First Empire "became the subject of serious academic history."[2] Datta also notes that there was, from the beginning, an "elasticity" to the Napoleonic legend that made it appealing to factions on both the political left and the right, assuring its longevity.[3]

Especially relevant to this essay are Datta's observations that "the most significant arena for the revival of the Napoleonic cult was in literature, in particular, the theatre, and in the fine arts," and that much of the literature on Napoleon published during the Belle Époque emphasized the private man and his personal relationships, rather than the public warrior and his military exploits.[4] For Frédéric Masson, Napoleon's biographer and probably the most prolific writer on Napoleon during this period, penetrating beyond the god-like hero in order to understand "his soul, his heart, his mind," and his passions as a son, lover, husband, and father, was a major aim of his work.[5] As Datta argues, "The historical scenes represented in the theater constituted popular, democratic history that bridged the distance between past and present by accentuating the personal attributes of public figures."[6] It is important to note here that the Belle Époque cult of Napoleon on the stage was only one manifestation of a widespread commercialism that speaks to the popular consumption of history in French society at the time.

Plays with Napoleonic themes—many of which explored the human side of this iconic figure—abounded on the Parisian stage. In 1893 alone, there were Victorien Sardou's *Madame Sans-Gêne*, Alphonse Lemonnier's *Madame la Maréchale*, Leopold Martin Laya's *Napoléon*, and Charles Grandmougin's *L'Empereur*; in 1899, Émile Bergerat's *Plus que Reine* and Émile Moreau's *Madame de Lavalette*; and in 1900, Edmond Rostand's *L'Aiglon* starring Sarah Bernhardt and a reprisal of *Madame Sans-Gêne*.[7]

Recreating period costumes was obviously an important aspect of these productions that treated such a significant era of French history. It was particularly true of *Plus que Reine* by the successful writer Émile Bergerat, a play in which Napoleon and Josephine were the main characters and which highlighted the coronation of 1804.[8] This essay focuses on the First Empire costumes that were integral to *Plus que Reine*'s narrative and were a compelling visual component for the ways in which they evoked these two famous historical figures, specifically in relation to well-known paintings of the Napoleonic period by Jacques-Louis David and Pierre-Paul Prud'hon. I also examine the longstanding influence of theatrical dress on women's fashion through the costumes worn by Jane Hading as Empress Josephine and the incipient Empire-revival vogue that was evident at the turn of the twentieth century. Throughout, I relate the play to the rise in study of French history that occurred over the course of the nineteenth century, a period during which theatrical, fashionable, and fancy dress reflected and participated in that history. Publications, plays, tableaux vivants, fancy dress balls, and fashion all contributed to the French collective historical imagination and to asserting a French national identity.[9]

Plus que Reine premiered at the Théâtre de la Porte-Saint-Martin on March 28, 1899, the same year in which Masson published his biography, *Joséphine, Impératrice et Reine*. Comments by reviewers of the play such as "We are in the midst of the Napoleonic legend"[10] and "Still him"[11] underscored the popularity of all things related to the emperor. In an interview with *Le Figaro* published on April 2, Bergerat noted that his characterization of Napoleon conformed to that of critical modern history, that is, of a "speaking, restless, living" man.[12] And indeed, the play's prologue and five acts focus on the "behind the scenes" human drama of the imperial couple's passionate, stormy relationship against the backdrop of momentous political events: their meeting in 1795 on the eve of the young general's suppression of a royalist insurrection;[13] Bonaparte's pardon of Josephine in 1799 (they were married in 1796) for deceiving him while he was on his Egyptian campaign; their coronation as emperor and empress in 1804; and the denouement in 1809 when a distraught Josephine finally agrees to sign a divorce decree so that Napoleon can remarry in order to produce an heir and secure his dynasty.

Reviews that appeared in the press were mixed regarding the work itself. Several critics questioned the suitability of the fifty-eight-year-old comedic actor Benoît-Constant Coquelin in the role of the emperor. A former member of the Comédie-Française and, in 1899, the director of the Porte-Saint-Martin, Coquelin was considerably older than Napoleon in the play: at the beginning, in 1795, he would have been twenty-six, and forty in 1809, at the end. However, an editorial in the May 1899 issue of *Le Théâtre* featuring the production insisted that the lack of physical resemblance between Coquelin and Napoleon—particularly their different profiles—was not an obstacle to the actor's portrayal of this historical figure: "The public asked only for the soul of the role. It got it. It seems happy."[14]

Indeed, the question of historical "truth" regarding representations of Napoleon on the stage was debated in the press. The writer Henry Fouquier, who reviewed Bergerat's play for *Le Figaro*, argued that there were two historical truths—the reality and the legend—and that, in the theatre, his preference was for reality. According to Fouquier, a literary work should convey either the legend, that is, the soul of a great man and the ideal that he represented, or the everyday person.[15] A few years earlier, however, Fouquier had been more accommodating of reconciling the "real" and "ideal" aspects of famous historical figures. Indeed, in terms of the literary phenomenon of the Napoleonic legend, including theatrical works, he claimed that the public was not necessarily interested in historical accuracy.[16] For French audiences, the theatre offered a reassuring legend of a great, if flawed, national hero rather than the harsh reality of Napoleon's defeat and exile.[17]

Across the editorial spectrum, however, critics widely lauded the production's impressive sets and, especially, the rich, faithfully copied costumes that recreated the sumptuous attire at the Napoleonic court. Notwithstanding his other criticisms of the play, Fouquier was favorably impressed by "the beauties of the work, admirably produced, with superb decors and dazzling costumes."[18] Although the plot focused on the intimate relationship between the emperor and empress, the historic episodes in which the story unfolded provided ample opportunity to display the full sartorial glory of the First Empire and, at the same time, to satisfy the contemporary fin-de-siecle theatrical taste for spectacle. Of all the Belle Époque plays that explored the Napoleonic theme, *Plus que Reine* was probably the most lavish in terms of the numbers and opulence of its costumes.

The elaborate mise-en-scène was fully recorded in the May 1899 issue of *Le Théatre*, an expensive, heavily illustrated monthly publication.[19] *Le Théatre* was one of many new theatre magazines that flourished in the late nineteenth and early twentieth centuries, particularly after the advent of half-tone printing, which allowed for the inclusion of text and image on the same page.[20] A colored photo engraving of Jane Hading as Empress Josephine in her coronation costume appears on the cover, and the interior pages contain a scene-by-scene plot summary, an editorial, acknowledgements by Bergerat, numerous full- and half-page black and white photographs, as well as two additional colored photoengravings of Benoît Coquelin as Napoleon and his son, Jean-Constant Coquelin, as Charles Maurice de Talleyrand-Périgord, Napoleon's Grand Chamberlain (see figures 1.1–1.3).

The photoengraving of Coquelin as Napoleon shows him in the emperor's quintessential military uniform of a Colonel of the Foot Grenadiers of the Imperial Guard. Jacques-Louis David, the official court painter, depicted Napoleon in this uniform in his well-known portrait *The Emperor Napoleon in his Study at the Tuileries* (1812, National Gallery of Art, Washington, D.C). In addition to the uniform, Coquelin/Napoleon wears a bicorne and a long, grey overcoat, two other items of dress strongly associated with the emperor.[21] By far, the majority of images of Napoleon depict him in military garb, identifying him as a soldier, a member of the Grande Armée, rather than an all-powerful ruler in ceremonial dress. In the years after his downfall, the components of Coquelin/Napoleon's costume became visual shorthand to convey the emperor.

Bergerat's notes on the mise-en-scène praise those responsible for realizing the sets and costumes. The latter, by Désiré Chaineux, the highly regarded in-house designer at the Comédie-Française, were fabricated by leading costumiers whom Bergerat gratefully acknowledges: "The house of Goupy, whose workers Arachne envies . . . executed the six toilettes worn successively by Madame Jane Hading and that all the newspapers in the world have described as marvels. . . . M. Muelle embroidered all Coquelin's costumes, including that for the coronation, a prodigious monument of his art, and whose reproduction is worthy of a display case in a museum of sovereigns."[22] Bergerat also credits Maison Pascaud and Maison Bauer-Ertzbischoff for the costumes worn by other characters, the firm of Gupterle et Broit for the jewelry, and Charles Aimé for the coiffures.[23] Several of these establishments advertised regularly in theatrical periodicals of the turn of the century.[24] Although Bergerat does not cite her, the well-known milliner Madame Carlier designed the hats and headdresses for Jane Hading. The actress patronized Madame Carlier beginning in the late 1890s, for millinery to wear with both her street dress and stage costumes.[25] Carlier's shop was located on the prestigious Rue de la Paix and editorials showcasing her creations—both fashionable and

Figure I.I. Cover of the May 1899 issue of *Le Théatre* showing Jane Hading as the Empress Josephine in her coronation costume. Author's collection.

theatrical—appeared frequently in several fashion periodicals at the turn of the century, including *L'Art et la Mode* and *Le Moniteur de la Mode*. Couturiers and milliners took full advantage of the visibility and free advertising that the stage offered, and society women eagerly sought out the latest ensembles that they had seen in the theatre from these leading fashion houses.

THÉATRE DE LA PORTE-SAINT-MARTIN
PLUS QUE REINE
Napoléon Bonaparte : M. Coquelin.

Figure 1.2. Benoît-Coquelin as Napoleon Bonaparte in the uniform of a colonel of the Foot Grenadiers of the Imperial Guarde. Author's collection.

THÉÂTRE DE LA PORTE-SAINT-MARTIN
PLUS QUE REINE
Talleyrand : M. Jean Coquelin.

Figure 1.3. Jean-Constant Coquelin as Charles-Maurice de Talleyrand-Périgord, Napoleon's Grand Chamberlain. Author's collection.

Bergerat's suggestion that Muelle's reproduction of Napoleon's coronation robes be displayed in "a museum of sovereigns" points to a perceived equivalency between the actual garments worn in 1804 and the copies worn onstage in 1899. Indeed, Bergerat may have been referring to the former Musée des Souverains, located in the Louvre, which was opened in 1852 by Louis-Napoleon and closed in 1872. One of its five galleries displayed objects that had belonged to Napoleon I and the King of Rome.[26] Executed at the highest levels of craftsmanship and with the finest materials, *Plus que Reine's* theatrical costumes could, it seems, stand in for the real thing and even become part of a historical narrative. Additionally, Bergerat's glowing recognition of the skilled needlework artisans who produced the "dazzling" costumes speaks to the exceptionally high regard in which the French luxury trades related to dress had long been held, trades that remained a source of great national pride. Just as Napoleon commissioned the most renowned embroiderer of his day—the firm of Picot—to embellish the official imperial costumes, so Bergerat engaged one of the most prestigious costumiers in late nineteenth-century Paris to create "authentic" copies of those garments.[27] As Bass-Krueger observes, the goal of designers like Chaineux and costumiers like Muelle was to create an illusion "in which theatrical costumes presented themselves as plausible fictions of past dress."[28]

As Bergerat states in his plot summary, the "culminating point" of *Plus que Reine's* third act was the tableau vivant of Jacques-Louis David's *The Consecration of Napoleon and the Coronation of Empress Josephine on December 2, 1804* (1805–7, Musée du Louvre).[29] The play's title refers to a prediction made by a fortuneteller to the young Marie-Josèphe-Rose Tascher de la Pagerie on her native island of Martinique, that one day she would be "plus que reine," more than queen. The oracle came true in December 1804 when Napoleon himself crowned her empress in a spectacular ceremony at Notre-Dame. Although nineteenth-century French theatregoing audiences were increasingly aware of and demanded historical accuracy in stage costumes, most plays set in the past (even those that may have treated subjects from French history) did not deliberately refer to recognizable images. Bergerat, thus, was faced with a particularly difficult task due to the public's familiarity with David's monumental canvas. As he explained in his notes on the mise-en-scène: "The main decorative 'key' of the work was the animated reconstruction of David's masterpiece, that everyone can admire . . . in the Louvre Museum. . . . The magnificent display of richness of court costumes, streaming with gold, jewels, brocades, satins and lace, all this ceremonial dress of splendor and dazzle . . . presented the problem of a tableau vivant all the more difficult to resolve because the public can see the model every

Figure 1.4. Jacques-Louis David, *The Consecration of Napoleon and the Corona-tion of the Empress Josephine on December 2, 1804* (1805–1807), Musée du Louvre. Art Resource.

day."[30] Bergerat also describes the set that recreated the interior of Notre-Dame as a "tour de force" by M. Carpezat and the impact of the coro-nation scene when it emerged from the shadows: "Each evening, there is a cry [from the audience]."[31]

Clearly, the costumes and set of Bergerat's tableau vivant succeeded in bringing to life David's *Consecration*—and literally inserted the audience into one of the most memorable events in French history. Theatregoers at the Porte-Saint-Martin "witnessed" the coronation of Josephine from David's vantage point in the cathedral's nave. *Plus que Reine* was a prime example of the plays performed in the "boulevard theater [in which] his-tory was made into a spectacle that could be consumed by socially di-verse audiences."[32] The "culminating point" of Bergerat's play also at-tests to the broader consumption of spectacle in the form of tableaux vivants, panoramas, and wax museums (available to the public in venues such as the Musée Grévin in Paris) that were enormously popular in late nineteenth-century France.[33]

Désiré Chaineux was certainly the ideal designer for the imperial court costumes. In his position at the Comédie-Française, which regu-larly staged historical plays, he would have had ample experience in cre-ating costumes from a wide range of periods, from antiquity to the eigh-teenth century. Indeed, his business card identifies him as "Designer of

Figure 1.5. Tableau vivant from *Plus que Reine*, act 3, mirroring David's *Consecration . . . .* Author's collection.

archaeology, Research for artists, history painter, Specialty in designs of historic costumes."[34] In his notes, Bergerat refers to the "infallible talent of a master such as M. Chaineux" that resulted in the scrupulous "details of the magnificent costuming."[35] A newspaper article that appeared two days after the play's opening also complimented his efforts for *Plus que Reine*. The reviewer, who had obviously seen Chaineux's drawings, noted, "As for the costumes, they have been designed by M. Chaineux, the very erudite designer of the Comédie-Française. That is to say that they will be of a meticulous exactitude as well an extreme variety. The play . . . covers a period of almost fifteen years, during which the uniforms often changed in form and color. M. Chaineux has faithfully noted these transformations in his remarkable watercolors [of the designs] with which one could truly compose a splendid album of costumes of the Empire."[36] Chaineux's emphasis on his business card of history and archaeology as his expertise speaks to two related developments in nineteenth-century France: the theatre's increasing attention to historical accuracy in stage costumes and the emerging study of French dress history, both of which insisted on the importance of primary sources.[37] Additionally, according to the reviewer, an album of Chaineux's *theatrical* (my emphasis) designs could itself serve as a reliable source as it contained a valid record of imperial uniforms and attested to the degree of historical accuracy—or perceived accuracy—of late nineteenth-century stage costumes.

As noted, David's coronation painting was the primary source for Chaineux's designs, but he might also have studied portraits of the emperor in his regalia such as that by Baron François Gérard (1805, Musée du Louvre) or Jean-Auguste-Dominique Ingres's *Napoleon I on His Imperial Throne* (1806, Hôtel des Invalides). He may have consulted Jean-Baptiste Isabey's detailed designs, which were commissioned for the coronation and decreed official court attire in July 1804.[38] Additionally, he may have been familiar with textual sources such as Alphonse Maze-Sencier's *Les Fournisseurs de Napoléon Ier et des deux impératrices (The Purveyors of Napoleon I and the two empresses)*, published in 1893, and he may have looked at extant garments from the period in public or private collections.[39] The Union Centrale des Arts Décoratifs, founded in 1882, acquired a First Empire dress in 1889, and five additional First Empire dresses during the 1890s.[40]

Another potential source for Chaineux's research may have been the second-hand clothing market, likely not for imperial court wear, but perhaps for richly embellished early nineteenth-century formal suits and gowns. During the latter decades of the century, artists, theatrical costume designers, and collectors purchased historic garments as objects of study, to use as studio props, for inspiration, or to be worn onstage.[41] In the latter case, both authentic historic pieces and newly created costumes that evoked the past reinforced the French public's interest in history broadly and dress history specifically, particularly their own. As Maude Bass-Krueger notes, "The popular reception of historical costumes . . . helped images and attitudes about the French past percolate deeply into popular culture."[42]

Comparing the coronation costumes worn in the tableau of *Plus que Reine* with those in David's painting reveals that they are remarkably faithful. Although Chaineux clearly took some liberties, primarily with motifs and some of the colors, the shapes and types of the garments as well as their luxurious embellishment replicate the magnificent attire associated with one of the most significant events in French history, recorded by one its most famous painters. Both Coquelin/Napoleon and Hading/Josephine wear the "grand habillement" (full-court dress). For the emperor this comprised a gold laurel-leaf crown, red velvet robe embroidered with gold bees and lined in ermine, a gold-embroidered white silk tunic, lace cravat, white silk breeches and stockings, and gold-embroidered shoes. The empress wore a jeweled diadem, a white silk gown with embroidery and fringe similar to the emperor's tunic, a standing lace collar, and mantle matching that of the emperor.[43] A review of the play in *Le Moniteur de la Mode* noted, "The tableau of the coronation is an enormous success. It is a reproduction of David's painting which is at Versailles. Napoleon and Josephine each wear the beautiful red velvet mantle with gold bees, fully lined with ermine, that David so marvelously depicted. The jewels worn by Mme Hading are clearly those that the painting shows us, including the fatal crown, too heavy for her forehead."[44] For Hading's costume, Chaineux added a train to the dress, likely for effect, and although the upper sleeves are puffed as in Isabey's design and David's painting, they do not have the same false slashing edged with diamonds that referenced late fifteenth-century dress. In spite of these differences, Hading/Josephine's costume would have been immediately recognizable to the audience as her coronation garb.[45]

Other figures in David's painting include the emperor's siblings and his in-laws and members of the royal household. In *Plus que Reine*'s tableau vivant, their costumes are also very similar to those seen in the canvas and follow Isabey's designs for court dress worn by princes, princesses, and officers of the crown (see figure 1.6).[46] Ensembles for women were closely based on Josephine's, incorporating an embroidered silk gown, standing lace collar, and velvet train. Ensembles for men were based on Napoleon's "petit habillement" (half-court dress), also designed by Isabey, which he wore to and from Notre-Dame, comprising a heavily gold and silver embroidered three-piece silk velvet and satin suit with additional historical flourishes of matching cape and plumed black felt hat.[47] In his costume for Jean-Constant Coquelin, who played Charles-Maurice de Talleyrand-Périgord, Chaineux deviated from the official scarlet color established by Isabey for Talleyrand in his position as "grand chambellan"; instead, Coquelin's court suit was blue with silver embroidery (see figure 1.3).[48]

Probably the most evident difference between the actual coronation clothing and the stage costumes is the scale of the embroidery. Consistent with theatrical garments that need to be "read" from a distance, the embroidered motifs are considerably larger and denser than those in the painting and those seen in extant garments: this is particularly true of the female characters' costumes. A First Empire–style dress designed by the eminent couturier Jacques Doucet in 1905 for an opera singer, now in the collection of the Palais Galliera, shows similar motifs (stylized foliage, meander pattern) and materials (silk satin, pearls, and gold and silver metal threads) that are exaggerated in their size and three-dimensionality.[49] On the other hand, the large-scale motifs seen in Chaineux's costumes for the male characters reflect Isabey's designs and David's painting, as well as surviving garments.

After Napleon's second abdication and exile in 1815, French military power diminished significantly and the army's humiliating defeat in the

THÉATRE DE LA PORTE-SAINT-MARTIN
PLUS QUE REINE
Acte III. 4ᵉ Tableau. — *La Famille corse.*

Figure 1.6. Scene from act 3 of *Plus que Reine* showing ensembles for the Imperial family and court. Author's collection.

Franco-Prussian War of 1870–71 still resonated with the French people at the end of the century. Venita Datta argues that the turn-of-the-century cult of heroes, of whom Napoleon was the ultimate exemplar, occurred in response to what the French public perceived as the mediocrity of their political leaders, and it further served to cement national solidarity and establish the Third Republic's legitimacy and roots in the past.[50] *Plus que Reine*'s striking tableau vivant of David's *Consecration* would have reminded audiences of the might and splendor of their imperial past and of Napoleon's revitalization of the luxury industries related to dress, and affirmed France's continued leadership in this particular realm.

In addition to attesting to the ubiquity of the Napoleonic legend at the turn of the century, *Plus que Reine* also demonstrates the theatre's longstanding influence on women's fashion and the role of actresses as trendsetters. Although, of course, both actors and actresses wore historicizing costumes onstage for plays set in the past, it was women's fashionable dress that regularly incorporated historicizing elements throughout the nineteenth century. This phenomenon was greatly enhanced in the century's latter decades by an ever-expanding fashion press and by the introduction of widely disseminated picture postcards with images of actresses.[51] Throughout the century, the many revival styles that found their way into women's fashion originated with or were given greater visibility by actresses' costumes.

Plus que Reine and other Napoleonic-themed plays were instrumental in popularizing late eighteenth- and early nineteenth-century styles and anticipating the full-blown Directoire-revival silhouette introduced by the couturier Paul Poiret in 1906.[52] In March 1900, *L'Art et la Mode* articulated the connection between the current vogue for high-waisted dresses with supple skirts inspired by those "that shone at the court of the great Emperor" and memories of the "epoch of Bonaparte awoken by the theatre,"[53] and fashion magazines of the period illustrated numerous examples of dresses and accessories designated "Directoire," "Consulat," and "Empire."[54]

Hading/Josephine's costume, in act 1's presentation of the first encounter between the fast-rising young General Bonaparte and the beguiling aristocratic widow six years his senior comprised a trained, columnar gown, a short jacket (known as a spencer in the early nineteenth century), a plumed "toque," and a long, Indian shawl (see figure 1.7). Chaineux based the ensemble on the dress of the so-called *merveilleuses,* the ultra-fashionable young women of the Directory, of whom Josephine was an acknowledged leader, a position she maintained during the Consulate and First Empire.

Within days of *Plus que Reine*'s opening, *L'Art et la Mode* featured multiple illustrations of hats by Madame Carlier for Jane Hading "inspired by paintings of the time," including "the delicious chapeau Malmaison" with pink roses, a white feather, and a Chantilly lace veil and a "Toque Empire, inspired by the portrait of Josephine" (see figures 1.8 and 1.9).[55] In fact, the "chapeau Malmaison" was something of a misnomer since Hading wore it in the opening scene set in the Palais-Royal. *La Vie parisienne* also commented on Hading/Josephine's stylish hats, describing them as "exquisite documents of the epoch, recreated by Mme Carlier, with a feeling for art and perfect taste."[56] Although millinery styles changed from year to year during the period encompassed by the play, Carlier's designs, with their close-fitting crowns, small, rounded brims, floral trimming, and long veils, are consistent with fashionable hats of the Directory and Consulate. Like most nineteenth-century historicizing fashions, her hats interpreted, rather than directly copied, original models.

The Indian shawls that were part of Hading's ensembles in the Palais-

ACTE Iᵉʳ. — Iᵉʳ TABLEAU.

Figure 1.7. Jane Hading as Josephine Beauharnais in act 1 of *Plus que Reine*. Author's collection.

Figure 1.8. *L'Art et la Mode*; hats inspired by Jane Hading's ensembles in *Plus que Reine*. Author's collection.

Royal and Malmaison scenes also became a point of fashion, for which she was credited. Hading's costume for the latter scene (act 3, scene 3) was based on Pierre-Paul Prud'hon's well-known 1805 *Portrait of the Empress Josephine* that, like David's *Consecration*, still hangs in the Louvre (see figures 1.10 and 1.11). The painting depicts the quintessential simplicity and understated luxury of Josephine's taste. The empress's delicately embroidered white muslin gown is set off by a brilliant red Indian shawl, one of many that she had in her extensive wardrobe.[57] In June 1899, *Le Moniteur de la Mode* illustrated the "Josephine scarf" and described it as one of the novelties being launched that season, inspired by First Empire shawls and revived by Jane Hading in Bergerat's play. The illustration shows the "Indian cashmere" shawl with "obligatory palmette motifs" worn with the mainstream S-curve silhouette rather than an Empire-style gown and trimmed with lace that gave it a "new allure," rather than the long fringe typical of early nineteenth-century Indian shawls.[58]

The *Moniteur*'s April review of *Plus que Reine* previously cited noted that Hading's "toilettes are sensational but they would not have any interest for our readers as they are richly formal gowns that one wouldn't know how to copy."[59] While it was certainly the case that the very heavy embroidery seen in Hading's coronation and other formal court costumes

Figure 1.9. Jane Hading as Josephine Beauharnais, wearing one of Mme Carlier's headpieces. Author's collection.

Figure 1.10. Pierre-Paul Prud'hon, *Portrait of the Empress Josephine* (1805), Musée du Louvre. Art Resource.

THÉÂTRE DE LA PORTE-SAINT-MARTIN
PLUS QUE REINE (ACTE III. — 3e Tableau)
Mme Jane Hading. — *Rôle de Joséphine.*
Toilette d'après le portrait de Prudhon (Musée du Louvre)

Figure 1.11. Jane Hading in her act 3, scene 3 costume, which was based on
Prud'hon's *Portrait of the Empress Josephine.* Author's collection.

Figure 1.12. *L'Art et la Mode*; empire-inspired evening gown. Author's collection.

was not imitated in fashionable dress, their slender shape and raised waistline are characteristic of Empire-revival modes illustrated in numerous fashion periodicals, and the delicate, metal thread embellishment of her "Prud'hon" gown had parallels in contemporary styles. In December 1899, *Le Moniteur de la Mode* pronounced, "At this moment, it is the Empire style that dominates dresses. . . . We have seen at [the house of] King a ball gown in the pure *Empire* style, which must have been copied from one of the pretty toilettes which were the charm of the Court festivities under Napoleon I."[60] The editor added that to see an Empire-style gown at a ball, that is, in a private setting, was not surprising, but that Empire-inspired street wear clearly affirmed the current vogue for these fashions.[61] However, judging by the examples illustrated in fashion periodicals, this style was, initially, most prevalent in eveningwear (see figure 1.12). Leading couture houses such as Doucet and Redfern, which designed both stage and street dress for Jane Hading and other actresses, created overtly revivalist, formal gowns that were enthusiastically reported on by fashion magazines.[62]

Hading/Josephine's jeweled diadem—one of several formal headdresses that she wore—attests to the blurring between theatrical costume and fashion. The magazine *La Mode pratique* often showed images

Figure 1.13. Postcard of Jane Hading in costume as Josephine, wearing a jeweled diadem and barrette. Author's collection.

of unidentified actresses on a single page under the heading "Les Elégances de la Semaine" (The Elegances of the Week). In 1900, the year after the production of *Plus que Reine*, "Les Elégances" included a detail from a photograph of Jane Hading as Josephine among other images of actresses. The photograph had already been reproduced as both a cabinet card and a postcard (see figure 1.13). The magazine's caption describes the gold wheat sheaf diadem and pearl barrette, but it does not identify the actress or the role.[63]

It is important to note that in addition to the extensive illustrations and descriptions in the fashion press that indicate the vogue for First Empire styles around 1900, the expanding literature on French dress history during the Belle Époque produced several works that focused on or included the Napoleonic period, such as P. L. Jacob's *Directoire, Consulat et Empire. Mœurs et Usages, Lettres, Sciences et Arts. 1795–1815* (1885); John Grand-Carteret's *XIXe Siècle (en France): classes, mœurs, usages, costumes, inventions* (1893); Henri Bouchot's *Le Luxe français: L'Empire* (1892); *La*

Toilette à la Cour de Napoléon (1895); and, slightly later, Henri Vever's *La bijouterie française au XIXe siécle* (1906–8).[64] These illustrated texts, aimed at a general readership, offered a scholarly source of information on early nineteenth-century dress and undoubtedly increased the interest in fashions of that period.

Beyond these publications, the cult of Napoleon and information about the First Empire more broadly were diffused through mass media, including newspapers, magazines, cabinet cards, postcards, and advertisements (see figure 1.14). For those who attended Bergerat's play, the May 1899 issue of *Le Théâtre* would have served as a souvenir, a reminder of the splendid production and its imposing historical subject matter. Those who were unable to attend might nonetheless have enjoyed leafing through the many illustrations. The magazine was a testament to the rapidly burgeoning press at the end of the nineteenth century, aimed at a middle-class audience eager to demonstrate its cultural awareness. In the pages of the *Plus que Reine* issue, a mechanically reproduced photograph recorded Bergerat's tableau vivant, which recreated David's painting, which in turn recorded the coronation of Josephine. *Le Théâtre* celebrated the theatre as a site of popular consumption and was itself intended for consumption.

Costume clearly played a key role in Emile Bergerat's *Plus que Reine*. In presenting two of the most famous figures in recent French history as his protagonists, he and his designer Chaineux would have been fully aware of the audience's familiarity with the abundant visual representations of Napoleon and Josephine and the potency of dressing his characters after these images. The recreation of Napoleonic court attire based on well-known works of art enhanced the connection between the turn-of-the-century performers and their historical counterparts. And, by virtue of their similarity to and influence on contemporary fashions, Hading's costumes reinforced the link between the styles of 1800 and 1900.

As the twentieth century opened and the centenary of Napoleon's coronation approached, the First Empire was vividly present in French art, literature, and fashion. In bringing the very *personal* love story of Napoleon and Josephine to life onstage—"this tragedy in which love and ambition are bound up in heroic and extraordinary circumstances," as Bergerat described it—the playwright clothed them in their most *public* garb, with which they were—and are—indelibly associated.[65] Peter Mondelli argues that "'history' [should] be understood . . . as a cultural undertaking in which a society attempts" to understand itself "by examining and representing the past" and that in the nineteenth century, history "was practiced in the rituals of everyday life."[66] Certainly the stage, and plays with impressive historical costumes, like *Plus que Reine*, were

Figure 1.14. Postcard of a scene from act 5 of *Plus que Reine* titled "Les Larmes" (The Tears) with a photograph of Jane Hading as Josephine inset. Author's collection.

a powerful ritual by which French society in the late nineteenth century could recreate and understand its past.

Notes

1. Henry Fouquier, "Les Théâtres," *Le Figaro* (April 6, 1899): 4. "Napoléon, qui est à la mode." All translations are by the author.

2. Venita Datta, *Heroes and Legends of Fin-de-Siècle France: Gender, Politics, and National Identity* (Cambridge: Cambridge University Press, 2011), 110.

3. Ibid., 111.

4. Ibid., 110, 114–15.

5. Frédéric Masson, *Napoléon et les Femmes* (Paris: Paul Ollendorf, 1894), xxx, xxiii. "Ce qu'il faut connaître c'est son âme, son cœur, son esprit." Between 1889 and 1912, Masson published numerous works on Napoleon and Josephine including *Napoléon, lieutenant d'artillerie (1786–1791)* (1889); *Napoléon et Les Femmes* (1893); *Napoléon chez lui: la journée de l'empereur aux Tuileries* (1894); *Napoléon Ier (empereur des Français 1769–1821* (1895); *Cavaliers de Napoléon* (1896); *Marie Walewska (Les maîtresses de Napoléon)* (1897); *Joséphine, Impératrice et Reine* (1899); *Joséphine répudiée, 1809–1814* (1901); *Joséphine de Beauharnais* (1902); *Napoléon et son fils* (1904); *Napoléon dans sa jeunesse, 1769–1793* (1907); *Livre du sacre de l'empereur Napoléon* (1908); *Trianon sous Napoléon* (1910); and *Napoléon à Sainte-Hélène* (1912). Masson's publisher, Paul Ollendorf, also published Émile Bergerat's play: Émile Bergerat, *Plus que Reine, Drame en cinq actes et un prologue* (Paris: Librairie Paul Ollendorf, 1899).

6. Datta, *Heroes and Legends*, 115.

7. Ibid., 110–11. In 1900, *Le Théatre* devoted one of its April issues (no. 32) to *L'Aiglon* and one of its June issues (no. 36) to *Madame Sans-Gêne*, with the popular actress Réjane reprising the lead.

8. Émile Bergerat (1845–1923) was a well-known and prolific French poet, playwright, columnist, and art critic. He was married to the daughter of the French Romantic poet Théophile Gautier. Bergerat's numerous plays were performed at several of the major theatres in Paris, including the Théâtre-Français, the Théâtre de Cluny, the Théâtre de l'Odéon, and the Théâtre de Vaudeville. He was awarded the Legion of Honor in December 1899. https://fr.geneawiki .com/index.php/75056_-_Paris_-_L%C3%A9gion_d%27honneur (accessed July 13, 2017). On June 23, 1899, *Gil Blas Illustré* published an interview with Bergerat as part of a series on leading authors; see "Émile Bergerat Raconté par lui-même," *Gil Blas Illustré*, no. 25 (June 23, 1899): 6–7.

9. For an in-depth study of the rise of dress history in France and historicism in theatrical costume and fashionable dress, see Maude Bass-Krueger, "The Culture of Dress History in France: The Past in Fashion, 1814–1900" (PhD diss., Bard Graduate Center: Decorative Arts, Design History, Material Culture, 2016).

10. A. Vallin, "Plus Que Reine, Compte Rendu," *Le Photo-programme, Revue artistique illustrée* No. 23 (1899): unpaginated. "On est tout à la légende napoléonienne." In his review, Vallin also noted that the theatre was following di-

rectly in the footsteps of authors such as Frédéric Masson, who had created and sustained the Napoleonic movement.

11. Gaston Sénner, "Toujours lui! Napoléon au théâtre," *La Presse* (April 4, 1899): unpaginated.

12. Jules Huret, "Avant la première de "Plus que Reine," *Le Figaro* (April 2, 1899): 4. "Le Napoléon de Plus que Reine qui est celui de la critique historique moderne, parlant, remuant, vivant."

13. Bergerat set the scene of their meeting in the Palais-Royal, the epicenter of Parisian social life in the years just prior to the Revolution and of revolutionary activity beginning in July 1789. However, scholars concur that the couple likely met in the home of Paul Barras, one of the five Directors of the French Republic. See *Réunion des musées nationaux, Joséphine* (Paris: Réunion des musées nationaux-Grand Palais, 2014), 73.

14. "L'Interprétation de 'Plus que Reine,'" *Le Théatre*, no. 17 (May 1899), 13. "Le public, lui, ne demandait que l'âme du rôle. Il l'a eue. Il paraît content." In fact, Coquelin used makeup to create Napoleon's acquiline nose.

15. Fouquier, "Les Théâtres," 4.

16. Datta, *Heroes and Legends*, 115, 121–22. Datta notes (121) that Fouquier also wrote a play about Napoleon.

17. Ibid., 121.

18. Fouquier, "Les Théâtres," 4. "J'ai dit les beautés de l'œuvre, admirablement mise en scène, avec des décors superbes et des costumes éblouissants."

19. *Le Théatre*, published by Jean Boussod, Manzi, Joyant & Cie, first appeared in January 1898. From that date through December 1899, it was published monthly, and from January 1899, bimonthly. The title of the magazine on its cover consistently appeared without the circumflex on the letter "a." Interestingly, Frédéric Masson, Napoleon's biographer and a friend of Michel Manzi, one of the magazine's publishers, was listed as a member of the editorial board in an advertising insert in *Les Modes*, another Manzi publication, in December 1903.

20. See Michele Majer, "Staging Fashion, 1880–1920," in Michele Majer, ed., *Staging Fashion, 1880–1920: Jane Hading, Lily Elsie, Billie Burke* (New York: Bard Graduate Center, 2012), 35–37.

21. A uniform of the Colonel of the Foot Grenadiers, bicorne, and grey greatcoat worn by Napoleon are in the collection of the Musée Napoléon I, Fontainebleau. See Colombe Samoyault-Verlet, "The Emperor's Wardrobe," in *The Age of Napoleon, Costume from Revolution to Empire: 1789–1815*, ed. Katell Le Bourhis (New York: Metropolitan Museum of Art, 1989), figs. 203, 206.

22. Émile Bergerat, "Quelques Notes sur la Mise en Scène de Plus que Reine," *Le Théatre* (May 1899): unpaginated. "C'est la Maison Goupy, dont Arachné envie les ouvrières qui, pour la joie des dilettantes de l'élégance, exécuta les six toilettes successivement portées par Madame Jane Hading et que tous les journaux du monde ont décrites comme des merveilles qu'elles sont en effet à tous les yeux. Pendant ce temps, M. Muelle brodait tous les costumes de Coquelin, jusqu'à celui du Sacre, monument prodigieux de son art, et dont la reproduction vaut la vitrine d'un musée des souverains."

23. Ibid.

24. See, for example, *Le Monde Artiste*, no. 23 (June 9, 1901), 356. The advertisement for R. Gupterle includes the information "Fournisseurs des Théâtres de l'Opéra, du Français et des principaux Théâtres étrangers" (Purveyors of the Theatres of the [Paris] Opera, the Français, and the principal foreign Theatres). "Français" refers to the Théâtre-Français, another name for the Comédie-Française.

25. William DeGregorio, "Fashion," in Michele Majer, ed., *Staging Fashion, 1880–1920: Jane Hading, Lily Elsie, Billie Burke* (New York: Bard Graduate Center, 2012), 103–4.

26. Bass-Krueger, "The Culture of Dress History in France," 131–32.

27. Aileen Ribeiro, *The Art of Dress: Fashion in England and France, 1750–1820* (New Haven, CT: Yale University Press, 1995), 157.

28. Bass-Krueger, "The Culture of Dress History in France," 161–62. In Sénner's review of *Plus que Reine* cited in note 11, he describes the importance of the sets in this regard, noting that they contribute to providing the audience with "the illusion of reality" ("l'illusion de la réalité"). Sénner, "Toujours lui! Napoléon au théâtre," unpaginated.

29. Bergerat, "Compte Rendu Analytique . . . ," *Le Théâtre* (May 1899): 6. "il en marque le point culminant au troisième acte."

30. Émile Bergerat, "Quelques Notes Sur la Mise en Scène," unpaginated. "Le grand 'clou' décoratif de l'ouvrage était cette reconstitution animée du chef d'œuvre de David, tel que tout le monde peut l'admirer au Musée du Louvre dans le Salon carré de l'Ecole française. . . . Le magnifique déploiement de richesse des costumes de cour, ruisselants d'ors, de pierreries, de brocarts, de satins et de dentelles, tout cet apparat de faste et d'éblouissement . . . proposait ici le problème d'un tableau vivant d'autant plus difficile à résoudre que le public en a lui-même tous les jours le modèle sous les yeux."

31. Ibid. "Un tour de force de M. Carpezat, quand la vision du Sacre surgit des ténèbres, c'est chaque soir, un cri de toutes les poitrines. Je n'ai rien à dire là-dessus que toute la presse n'ait chanté."

32. Datta, *Heroes and Legends*, 115. Unlike the elitist, state-supported Comédie-Française, known for its classical repertoire, many of the boulevard theatres (like the Porte-Saint-Martin) specialized in melodramas and other "popular" genres that attracted a more mixed and particularly working-class audience.

33. Ibid., 115. Bass-Krueger also discusses the widespread popularity of this type of spectacle at World's Fairs and in museum exhibitions; see Bass-Krueger, "The Culture of Dress History," 117–19, 138–41.

34. Désiré Chaineux file, Bibliothèque de la Comédie-Française, Paris. "Dessinateur d'archéologie, Recherches pour artistes, peintre d'histoire, Spécialité de dessins de costumes historiques." The author would like to thank Maude Bass-Krueger for providing this information.

35. Bergerat, "Quelques Notes Sur la Mise en Scène," unpaginated. "C'était beaucoup déjà d'obtenir, et grâce au talent infaillible d'un maître tel que M. Chaineux, les moindres détails de cette costumation grandiose."

36. "Indiscrétions Théâtrales," *Gil Blas* (March 30, 1899): unpaginated.

"Quant aux costumes, ils ont été dessinés par M. Chaineux, le si érudit dessina-teur de la Comédie-Française. C'est dire qu'ils seront d'une exactitude méticu-leuse, en même temps que d'une variété extrême. La pièce est épisodique, comme on sait: elle embrasse une période de près de quinze années, pendant laquelle les uniformes ont changé bien souvent de forme et de couleur. M. Chaineux a fidèle-ment noté ces transformations dans ses aquarelles si remarquables, avec lesquelles on pourrait vraiment composer un splendide album de costumes de l'Empire."

37. See, especially, chapter 3, "Staging the Past: Historical 'Veracity' in Eugène Lacoste's Costumes for the Opéra de Paris, 1876–1892," in Bass-Krueger, "The Culture of Dress History in France," 152–204.

38. Madeleine Delpierre, "Le Retour aux costumes de cour sous le Consulat et l'Empire," in *Modes et Révolutions, 1780–1804* (Paris: Musée de la Mode et du Costume, Palais Galliéra, 1989), 36. See also Frédéric Masson, *Livre du sacre de l'empereur Napoléon* (Paris: Goupil & Cie; Manzi, Joyant & Cie, 1908). Masson's book includes color illustrations of Isabey's designs for official court dress.

39. Alphonse Maze-Sencier, *Les Fournisseurs de Napoléon Ier et des deux impéra-trices: d'après des documents inédits tirés* (Paris: H. Laurens, Librairie Renouard, 1893).

40. Email communication from the Centre de Documentation, Les Arts Dé-coratifs, Paris, June 24, 2013. The dress acquired in 1889 (Inv. 4600AB) is a formal silk satin dress with silk embroidery, though not an official court dress. It was purchased from Edmond Taigny, a collector and founding member of the Union Centrale des Arts Décoratifs. In 1908, the museum acquired two pairs of shoes that belonged to Josephine as well as two single shoes that belonged to Caroline Murat, one of Napoleon's sisters.

41. Bass-Krueger, *The Culture of Dress History*. Regarding the second-hand market, see 279–89; regarding mid- and late nineteenth-century collectors of his-toric clothing, see 101–9, 123–26.

42. Ibid., 154.

43. See Masson, *Livre du sacre*, plates 1 and 3. The imperial decree of July 18, 1804, for Josephine's grand habillement specifies "Robe de soie blanche sans queue" (White silk dress without a train); see the text accompanying plate 3 for *Grand Habillement de l'Impératrice* in Masson, *Livre du sacre,* unpaginated.

44. *Le Moniteur de la Mode* (April 22, 1899): 183. "Le tableau du sacre a un succès énorme. C'est la reproduction du tableau de David, qui est à Versailles. Napoléon et Joséphine portent l'un et l'autre le beau manteau de velours rouge aux abeilles d'or et tout doublé d'hermine, que David a si merveilleusement rendu. Les bijoux que porte Mme Hading sont bien ceux que le tableau nous montre, y compris la fatale couronne, trop lourde pour son front." Between 1808 and 1822, Jacques-Louis David painted a replica of his famous image, now in the collection in the Musée du Château de Versailles. http://ressources.chateauversailles.fr/Sacre-de-l-empereur-Napoleon-Ier-et-couronnement-de-l-imperatrice-Josephine (accessed June 6, 2017).

45. For examples of extant court costumes worn by Empress Josephine, see Claudette Joannis, *Joséphine, Impératrice de la Mode: L'élégance sous l'Empire* (Paris: Éditions de la Réunion des musées nationaux, 2007), figures 1 (p. 6), 20

(p. 34), 21 (p. 35), 22 (p. 36), figure 23 (p. 37), figure 42 (p. 66), and figure 43 (pp. 67–68).

46. Masson, *Livre du sacre*. See, for example, plates 6 (*Prince français*), 7 (*Princesse*), 8 (*Prince Grand dignitaire*), 9 (*Maréchal d'Empire portant les Honneurs*), and 10 (*Dame du Palais portant les Offrandes*).

47. Aileen Ribeiro, *The Art of Dress*, 162. The shape, construction, and decoration of the "petit habillement" were holdovers of the late eighteenth-century formal suit. Isabey's design for the "petit habillement" is reproduced in Masson, *Le Livre du Sacre*, plate 2.

48. See Pierre-Paul Prud'hon's portrait of Charles-Maurice de Talleyrand-Périgord in his uniform of *Grand Chambellan* (1807, Musée Carnavalet). See also the plate and accompanying text for the *Habillement d'un Grand Officier de la Couronne* in Masson, *Livre du sacre*, plate 12. As Grand Chambellan, Talleyrand's uniform was "écarlate" (scarlet).

49. Palais Galliera, Musée de la Mode de la Ville de Paris (accession number 86.138.8). According to the cataloguing information, the dress was worn by Mademoiselle Marthe Davelli.

50. Datta, *Heroes and Legends*, 123, 127.

51. See Majer, "Staging Fashion, 1880–1920," 31–35. See also the sections "In the Photographer's Studio," in the individual essays on Jane Hading, Lily Elsie, and Billie Burke.

52. Harold Koda and Andrew Bolton, *Poiret* (New York: Metropolitan Museum of Art; New Haven, CT: Yale University Press, 2007), 14.

53. *L'Art et la Mode* (March 24, 1900): 29. "Tous ces souvenirs de l'époque de Bonaparte réveillés par le théâtre, nous donnent le goût de ces robes si jolies, avec leur taille courte, leur jupe souple, qui brillèrent à la Cour du grand Empereur."

54. In 1899 and 1900, both *Le Moniteur de la Mode* and *L'Art et la Mode* illustrated dresses, short jackets, and hats with these descriptors.

55. *L'Art et la Mode* (April 8, 1899): 261, 270–71. "Coiffures inspirées des Tableaux du Temps créés pour Jane Hading dans *Plus que Reine* par Me Carlier 16 rue de la Paix" (coiffures inspired by paintings of the time created for Jane Hading in *Plus que Reine* by Me Carlier). "Délicieux chapeau Malmaison en Chantilly, mais à torsade . . . grappe de roses roses posée de côté . . . grande plume blanche" and "Toque Empire, inspirée du portrait de Joséphine." The latter is probably based on a portrait of the Empress Josephine by Pierre Louis Bouvier (1766–1836, ca. 1812), http://www.christies.com/lotfinder/Lot/pierre-louis-bouvier-geneva -1766-1836-portrait-4587478-details.aspx/. In addition to the portrait on canvas, Bouvier painted Empress Josephine in the same dress and similar pose in several miniatures.

56. *La Vie parisienne* (April 1, 1899): 180.

57. See *Réunion des musées nationaux, Joséphine* (Paris: Réunion des musées nationaux-Grand Palais, 2014): 40, and Serge Grandjean, *Inventaire après décès de l'Impératrice Joséphine à Malmaison* (Paris: Réunion des musées nationaux, 1964), 49, 51. The inventory includes shawls as well as garments made from shawls.

58. *Le Moniteur de la Mode* (June 10, 1899): 265. "Parmi les nouveautés qu'on

lance cette saison, citons l'écharpe *Joséphine,* inspirée de celle que l'on portait sous le premier Empire, et que Mme Hading a ressuscitée avec tant de charme dans sa nouvelle création de la Porte-Saint-Martin. C'est du cachemire de l'Inde, très léger, fond blond avec les obligatoires palmes kachemyr. Seulement, au lieu de franges à chaque extrémité, une jolie dentelle un peu lourde, donnant une allure très neuve à ce semblant de vêtement."

59. *Le Moniteur de la Mode* (April 22, 1899): 183. "Ses toilettes sont sensationelles, mais n'auraient aucun intérêt pour nos lectrices, car elles sont toutes des robes d'apparat ou de fantaisies qu'on ne saurait copier."

60. *Le Moniteur de la Mode* (December 9, 1899): 577, in "Chronique de la Mode." "En ce moment, c'est le genre Empire qui domine les robes et pour les vêtements. Nous avons vu chez King une robe de bal de pur style *Empire,* qui a dû être copiée sur l'une de ces jolies toilettes qui faisaient le charme des fêtes de la Cour sous Napoléon 1ᵉʳ."

61. Ibid. "Mais porter une robe Empire au bal, ce n'était rien. À la ville, c'est affirmer encore le gout que nous avons pour ces formes."

62. Majer, *Staging Fashion,* 99–103.

63. "La Mode pratique," no. 3 (1900): unpaginated. "Coiffure faite de deux gerbes de trois épis d'or formant diadème, avec barette de perles derrière." The page includes eight images of actresses (including Hading), some of whom are identified by their name and role (Mme Sorel in *Struensé,* Mme Bréval in *La Burgonde*).

64. P. L. Jacob, *Directoire, consulat et empire: mœurs et usage, lettres, sciences et arts: France, 1795–1815* (Paris: Firmin-Didot et Cie, 1885); *John Grand-Carteret, XIXe siècle en France: classes, mœurs, costumes, inventions, illustrations* (Paris: Firmin-Didot et Cie, 1893); Henri Bouchot, *Le Luxe français: L'empire* (Paris: Librairie illustrée, 1892); Henri Bouchot, *La Toilette à la cour de Napoléon, Chiffons et Politique de Grandes Dames (1810–1815)* (Paris: La Librairie illustrée, 1895); Henri Vever, *La Bijouterie française au XIX siècle (1800–1900)* (Paris, H. Floury, 1906–1908).

65. Huret, "Avant la première de 'Plus que Reine,'" 4. "Cette tragédie où l'amour et l'ambition sont aux prises dans des conditions heroïques et extraordinaires."

66. Peter Mondelli, "The Sociability of History in French Grand Opera: A Historical Materialist Perspective," in *19th Century Music* 37, no. 1 (Summer 2013): 43.

Creating a Realistic

Rendering Pedagogy

The Fashion Illustration Problem

Caitlin Quinn

A CHALLENGING BUT CRUCIAL STEP in the costume design process is creating the rendering. This drawn representation of the costume design can be a work of art, but it also must convey crucial information to the director and production team: namely, what is the costume and how will it fit the actor and the character? This can confound beginning designers, who often want to draw beautiful interpretations of their designs on the perfect model, which does not always reflect the actor. However, the body that wears the costume is an important part of the design process. In this paper, I explore the challenges and successes of creating a pedagogy focused on the costume designer's depiction of the actor's body in the rendering. For my costume rendering course, I created projects to challenge the student's sense of realistic representation versus artistic interpretation, and to address the value of rendering diverse bodies as part of the design process.

As the professor of costume design at the University of South Dakota, I teach undergraduate designers in the courses Costume Design and Advanced Costume Design. However, I was inspired to create a new course called Advanced Costume Rendering after observing that the costume design students were lacking in rendering body diversity and dynamic poses. Students were not considering the vastly different types of actor bodies, and most only had the confidence to render in a one-size-fits-all model. I noticed that undergraduate design students were not paying attention to the body wearing the costumes they had meticulously designed. They wrote thoughtful character analyses, but the character wasn't coming across on the rendering page. Instead, the costumes were rendered on fashion figures. Before the costume is added, the figure drawn in the rendering must accurately convey the body shape of the actor and the attitude of the character through stance. This gives the director a real sense of how the costume will fit the actor and contribute to the audience's perception of the character. Because of these complexities in costume rendering, the simplicity of fashion illustration style is attractive to beginning designers. Fashion illustration represents an idealized drawing of the human form and does not display a developed character. Students are often drawn to the idealized human form and straightforward body positioning used in fashion illustration instead of rendering the actor's actual body type or expressive poses. Rendering this way is easier because once the designer masters drawing the idealized body, it can be repeated for each rendering instead of adjusting for individual actor size.

Teaching students the diversity of the human form and the importance of characterization in poses is an integral part of costume rendering. Students draw better representations of realized garments on actors when they first focus on the body, and character, that the costume is being put upon. A rendering curriculum needs to encourage students to celebrate actor body diversity and realize the importance of rendering the character to enhance their design concept. As the theatre community is seeing more productions that include and celebrate actors of all sizes and races, it is important that young designers learn to reflect that diversity at the planning stage of the design process. Costume designers should enter the professional world comfortable with rendering actors who look different from themselves or the ideal fashion body.

I decided to create a rendering course that would devote time to the body as part of the rendering. The objectives for Advanced Costume Rendering were to introduce students to the standard human form, encourage students to adjust for actor size, familiarize students with rendering diverse races, and promote dynamic character positioning in costume renderings. These objectives better familiarized students with the purpose of costume design versus fashion illustration and resulted in a closer study of the actor's body and character attitude as part of the design.

In my Costume Design I course, I noticed that beginning costume designers were often drawing tall, slender figures in neutral poses for every character they rendered. The students worked on unrealized paper projects without a cast, but the scripts I assigned them would call for characters of specific sizes and big personalities. Much of the characterization was lost in their renderings because of the use of the idealized body and front-facing, presentational poses. These designers were using fashion croquis, stock body outlines that the designer traces and draws clothing onto, for convenient figures upon which to render the costume. Popular in fashion illustration, croquis are described as "faceless, doll-like, almost androgynous fashion illustration figures [that] express the same effect in providing an instructional model for students."[1] The idealized figure used in fashion croquis is "a tall . . . slender, athletic young woman. She has a small bosom and broad shoulders, so clothes hang easily over her lithe silhouette. . . . Her face, hair and body have a natural look."[2] The figure does not represent a character with a distinct personality, but an aspirational body for the fashion consumer. Conversely, actors are cast because they do not conform to the "ideal" body type, but rather an appropriate type for the character. "Actors come in all shapes and sizes. In fact, body type is often an important factor when it comes to casting decisions. Theatre, film and television need a wide variety of types of bodies, so *vive la différence!*"[3] Since physical features are an important factor in casting, students need to showcase these diverse actor bodies in their renderings.

Croquis are a convenient crutch for students learning how to draw, but the figures are often distorted, with elongated legs and tiny waists. For introductory design courses, carefully selected croquis with realistic proportions may help students with no previous drawing experience. However, for students pursuing a career in costume design, as most of the Advanced Costume Rendering students were, croquis of any kind promote an idealized form if not adjusted for the actor's body type. The perpetuation of the fashion illustration style in costume rendering may lead to miscommunication between actors and directors as to what the final costume will look like on the performer's body, whereas the costume rendering that successfully synthesizes actor and character is a true vision of the design for actors and directors.

A successful figure in costume design represents the actor's true height, weight, race, and interpretation of the character. The same set of student designers from Costume Design 1 took my Advanced Costume Rendering course. These were mostly students pursuing a BFA in Costume Design, and several others focused in other design areas. The Advanced Rendering course was created for these students to develop the drawing skills necessary for a career as a professional costume designer. I began the course by tackling realistic standard body proportions, as opposed to the elongated fashion proportion. When using the human head as a unit of measurement, the fashion figure is between nine and ten heads tall, while the average human is around seven and a half heads tall. The class used the textbook *Anatomy: A Complete Guide for Artists* by Joseph Sheppard, to draw the classical human figure, which is eight heads tall and two heads wide at the hips and shoulders. The classical body is divided with a four-head length above the pelvic bone and four-head length below the pelvic bone.[4] Students drew a fashion figure and a classical figure, and then measured themselves (using the head unit of measurement) and drew their own figure in proportion. The differences between all three bodies were striking. Some students had longer torsos, some longer legs, and no one was a perfect eight heads tall. The objective of this activity was for students to recognize the significance of adjusting the body in the rendering to the specific actor. The students enjoyed the project because the proportional concepts made better sense when related directly to their own bodies. One petite student measured herself at six and a half heads tall and narrow at the hips and shoulders. She connected this to her tendency to draw all her figures as slim waifs.

It is important that the designer uses the actor's real body at the rendering stage, since that is when the garment is initially designed. If a generic stock body is used for every female character in the production, the designer misses the opportunity to better flatter different skin tones and proportions. Another consideration is the actor's possible discomfort in the costume if it was not designed with their body in mind. When confronted with the rendering, the actors should see themselves as the characters and not idealized versions of themselves wearing the character's clothing. An actor may be more comfortable and confident when first trying on their costume if they more closely resemble the sketch. A costume that is rendered on the ideal fashion figure, ten heads tall and slim, will look different when constructed for an actor that is seven heads tall with a less fit build. A sketch with idealized proportions sets up unrealistic expectations for the actor when they put on the realized costume. In *Costume: Performing Identities Through Dress*, Pravina Shukla describes an experience costume designer Rafael Jaen had with idealized renderings and real actor bodies: "Once he met the actor, he realized that she did not actually resemble the celebrity and that the costume he had sketched would be wholly wrong for her. But by this stage in the process the director of the play had become attached to Rafael's original design. Rafael noticed that the actor herself was uncomfortable with being asked to wear such a revealing costume that . . . would flatter only someone with a toned body."[5] The effect an idealized rendering can have on an actor is like the effect garments seen on runway models can have on consumers when they try them on at the retail store: disappointment. In addition, not changing the figure proportions for each character saves time, but it sacrifices an opportunity for the designer to sell the director their vision for the character as portrayed by that specific actor. In *The Art and Practice of Costume Design*, Stephen Stines explains, "The actors cast in a show . . . will hopefully be in good shape and know how to wear clothes, but they are still human beings, and, as noted, part of the goal of the costume sketch is to work out the proportions of clothing in relation to the body on which it will be seen."[6] When the designer sketches the real human behind the costume they will produce a better design because the costume will be specific to that actor as well as the character.

To practice adjusting the figure to a real actor's unique body shape, the students were tasked with designing costumes for four characters in Peter Raby's stage adaption of *The Three Musketeers*, using real people as the actors. The students had to cast these characters with people from their own lives and render to match the actors' body types. The project taught students that an appropriately sized figure affects how the costumes are designed and will result in more flattering garments in realized productions. Some of the students asked to measure their actors using the head system to more accurately render their bodies. While this would not usually be workable in the professional world, I allowed the students to do it for this project as they were still developing their eye for proportion. None of the students resorted to croquis for this project, and the most successful designs were the ones for which the students photographed and measured the actors.

Even after *The Three Musketeers* project, when the students were asked to design for uncast productions, they often chose to render figures who were Caucasian and slim. Seven of the eight students in the class were Caucasian and only one student was male. Most of these students had trouble drawing nonwhite figures or large male figures because they were so different from their own bodies. In *Drawing and Rendering for Theatre: A Practical Course for Scenic, Costume, and Lighting Designers*, Clare P. Rowe describes how perception of our own bodies affects how we instinctively render the human form: "Because we are intimately familiar with our own bodies, this intuitive knowledge of what each of us looks like acts as a detriment when attempting to draw a specific individual human form. . . . By adulthood the imagery in our minds of the human form is so iconic that, when attempting to draw accurately from life, it requires concentrated effort to ignore our stored symbolic image memories of the human form."[7] Beyond their own bodies, many of the students in the class drew inspiration from fashion media for their renderings and the fashion world reinforced their worldview rather than challenging it. The models who walked the runway for the Fall 2015 fashion season were 80 percent Caucasian (this includes casting in New York, London, Paris, and Milan shows),[8] and there were no plus-size or "brawny" male models represented in Fall 2016 runway shows.[9] Conversely, the Asian American Performers Action Coalition released a survey for the 2014/2015 Broadway theatre season, which found that "there is a definite upward trend in the casting of actors of color. For the first time, 30 percent of all available roles went to actors of color, a jump from 24 percent the previous year."[10] Additionally, at the University of South Dakota, some of the actors the students work with would be considered plus-size by fashion standards. Students reported some anxiety about rendering different ethnicities and sizes because they did not want to offend the actor if the rendering inadvertently overexaggerated features or size. I explained that one purpose of the class was to provide a safe space to practice realistic body rendering before using it in realized productions.

To get the students more comfortable with diversity in their renderings, first they read sections from chapters 2 and 3 of Tan Huaixiang's excellent book *Character Costume Figure Drawing*, which has examples of facial features of different races and weight distribution of different body types. Second, the students were given specific, successful, professional actors whose body type and/or race were far from the type the student tended to draw. They were asked to render the actors, paying careful attention to their facial structure and body size. A student who gravitated toward fit men and thin models for figures was challenged to draw Octavia Spencer, an Oscar-winning plus-size African American actress. Another student, who consistently overelongated all her figures, was given actor Peter Dinklage, a little person, to challenge her perception of proportion. Finally, a student who drew her inspiration for male figures from slender male runway models was given the brawny actor Dwayne Johnson as her model. The objective of the project was for students to confront their own ideas of the ideal human body, identify how it was affected by the fashion industry and their own appearance, and grow more comfortable depicting diverse bodies in rendering. It took the students longer to plot out the figure proportions since the actors were different sizes than those they were used to sketching, but overall the students embraced the challenge. The more difficult step was rendering the actor's faces to reflect their age and ethnicity. The students who were most successful at this task applied the "less is more" method. They picked the most striking features about the actor (large eyes, wide mouth, narrow nose) and focused on those instead of cramming too much detail into the small drawing space. The focus on features as well as proportion led into the body rendering project about drawing an expressive figure.

The final step in teaching a realistic body rendering style was to examine the importance of rendering the figure as an expressive character. While both fashion illustrations and costume renderings need to display the garment design on the body, the communicative role of the body differs between the mediums. In fashion illustration, the body helps to express the attitude of the clothing: "The pose should be relevant to the context of the clothing (for example, it would make little sense to draw a sporty pose for a wedding dress or an evening gown)."[11] In costume rendering, the actor dictates the body shape, the character dictates the body position, and the clothing supports the context of the text and production. For example, a character may need to fight in an evening gown so the figure rendered is less demure and more active, in a sporty pose. The costume designer is challenged to present a complete character through clothing design and figure position. The more accurately the rendering reflects the actor's body shape and the character's attitude, the more clearly the production team can see the transformation from actor to character in relation to the total world of the production. In *Character Costume Figure Drawing*, Tan Huaixiang explains her rendering process: "When I create costume designs, I try not only to illustrate the costumes, but also to portray a completed characterization. . . . People say that we should not judge a person by his or her appearance, but when an actor appears onstage, his or her appearance becomes significant. The character's body language reflects the soul and spirit of the character."[12] The model drawn in a fashion illustration acts as a neutral hanger for the clothing, whereas the actor is a dynamic, moving inhabitant of the costume, projecting a character to the audience.

The practical style of rendering the actor's body and character instead of a fashion figure is a relatively modern development in costume design and can be tied to the emergence of costume design as a specific discipline in theatre education in the late twentieth century.[13] To understand the importance of rendering characters in costume design, the students were first tasked with rendering a historical garment or haute couture fashion outfit on a figure of their choice. Most of the students chose presentational front facing positions or fashion style figures in a "runway walk" with blank expressions. The outfits had a lot of attitude, but without a character behind the seams, the renderings were devoid of emotion. I then presented the students with Gregg Barnes's renderings for *Disney's Aladdin on Broadway* as a good example of character attitude and body position. I chose Barnes's work because it is a recent show that most of the students were familiar with, and his character positions are not overly exaggerated yet are still emotive. When juxtaposed with their own renderings, students found the expressiveness of Barnes's figure's faces and poses more appealing.

Then, the students were assigned to render four characters from *The Three Musketeers*. As noted, they were required to cast the production with real people to accurately render the actor body. Additionally, the characters they tackled (d'Artagnan, Milady, Constance, and Cardinal Richelieu) are all over-the-top characterizations of heroes or villains. The archetypal nature of the characters allowed the students to distill their personalities down to a simple title: hero, seductress, damsel in distress, or villain. The simplified characters made it easier for the students to come up with poses to express their personality. As an example, they looked at Disney villains' and heroes' poses from the animated films— no subtlety there. The objective for this project was for students to pay extra attention to how the body was positioned in the rendering to best express the character. Their goal was that anyone who looked at the rendering would be able to deduce a bit about the character's personality.

The students' work was successful, especially with the male hero and villain figures. The students found the femme fatale and damsel in distress characters harder to position expressively because of the period garments. An unexpected benefit of the project was that it opened a class discussion about historical costumes for modern audiences. Students struggled with how to render a seductive pose when the character had to wear a long skirt and corset. They were challenged to synthesize what would be a seductive position in sixteenth-century France with what the modern director would see as seductive. After this project, the assigned scripts dealt with more complicated characters so the body positions became less dynamically posed as the students struggled to present the characters in one snapshot. However, few reverted back to the neutral fashion stances previously favored.

As the class moved on from the body rendering projects, statuesque model figures graced the student's sketchbooks less and less and were replaced by more recognizable forms. After the rendering diversity projects, students were more willing to draw different body types and ethnicities for paper projects when the actors were not specified. Students paid closer attention to actual actor size for projects when the actors were specified. Although students still reverted to fashion poses and neutral expressions when pressed for time, many did tackle characterization in renderings when given a longer work period. Overall, the focus on the actor's body and character pose as an important part of the rendering produced better design work from the students. The body in their renderings became more than a hanger: it became the actor, the character, and the part of the complete design.

The costume design students will eventually graduate and move into the professional world of design. The projects they tackled in Advanced Costume Rendering will better prepare them to confidently embrace a diversifying artistic community with a sense of familiarity rather than a fear of the unknown. By acknowledging the importance of the actor's body, these designers will help create a more inclusive theatrical space, beginning at the start of the design process: the rendering.

Notes

1. Donna R. Danielson, "The Changing Figure Ideal in Fashion Illustration," *Clothing and Textiles Research Journal* 8, no. 1 (1989): 12.

2. Mona Shafer Edwards and Sharon Lee Tate, *The Complete Book of Fashion Illustration* (New York: Pearson, 1982).

3. Steven Breese, *On Acting: A Handbook for Today's Unique American Actor* (Indianapolis: Hackett Publishing, 2013), 142.

4. Joseph Sheppard, *Anatomy: A Complete Guide For Artists* (New York: Dover Publications, 1992), 12–17.

5. Pravina Shukla, *Costume: Performing Identities Through Dress* (Bloomington: Indiana University Press, 2015), 217.

6. Stephen Stines, "Costume Rendering," in *The Art and Practice of Costume Design*, ed. Melissa L. Merz (New York: Routledge, 2017), 127.

7. Clare P. Rowe, *Drawing and Rendering for Theatre: A Practical Course for Scenic, Costume, and Lighting Designers* (Burlington, VT: Focal Press, 2013), 38.

8. Jessica Andrews, "Despite Gains, the Fall 2016 Runways Were Still Less Than 25 Percent Diverse (Report)," *Fashion Spot*, March 16, 2016, http://www.thefashionspot.com/runway-news/685109-runway-diversity-report-fall-2016/.

9. Lauren Chan, "These Were All the Plus-Size Model Appearances at Fashion Month Fall 2016," *Glamour*, March 3, 2016, http://www.glamour.com/story/plus-size-models-fashion-month-fall-2016.

10. Robert Viagas, "Coalition Releases Report on Diversity in NY Theatre," *Playbill*, May 3, 2016, http://www.playbill.com/article/coalition-releases-report-on-diversity-in-ny-theatre.

11. John Hopkins, *Fashion Drawing* (Lausanne: AVA, 2010), 56.

12. Tan Huaixiang, introduction to *Character Costume Figure Drawing* (Waltham, MA: Focal Press, 2004), vii.

13. Melissa L. Merz, "The Magic of Costume Design," in *The Art and Practice of Costume Design*, ed. Melissa L. Merz (New York: Routledge, 2017), 73.

Where'd I Put My Character?

The Costume Character Body and Essential Costuming for the Ensemble Actor

Aly Renee Amidei

For 'tis your thoughts that now must deck our kings.
—Shakespeare, *Henry V*, prologue

IN A SMALL THEATRE housed in a former Commonwealth Edison substation on the North Side of Chicago, ten actors are trying to bring *Treasure Island* to life on Lifeline Theatre's stage. The actor playing Captain Flint runs offstage, removes his captain's coat, takes a deep breath, and sips from his water bottle. He has one whole page before he has to come back as Israel Hands in the next scene. Then he hears his cue line. "What the . . . ? They skipped a page!" He looks around frantically: "Where'd I put my character?" The assistant stage manager points to a black thing on the floor. Relieved, the actor puts on Israel's eye patch and dashes to his next entrance just in time. "Yarr!"

Chicago storefront theatres, as exemplified by Lifeline Theatre, regularly cast a small ensemble of actors to play multiple roles. When a company produces an ambitious play with a small cast, distinguishing between multiple characters becomes an opportunity for discovery between the director, costume designer, and the actor. When the additional challenges of budget, space, blocking, and time are factored in, sometimes the only visual indication between shifting characters comes down to a single garment or costume prop. The manner in which these tangible pieces are determined and the way they then inform both the work of the actor and audience reception are excellent ways to reflect on the powerful relationship of the performer and the costume. This essay examines the function of costume within this type of production model. Further, it looks at the manner in which costume becomes a type of body to be worn by the actor, and the way in which the multiple "costume bodies" worn by an ensemble actor create a composite body that contributes added meaning for the audience. Additionally, best practices for costuming an ensemble actor are outlined and explored.

The majority of the non-Equity and smaller Equity theatre companies of Chicago produce in spaces converted for performance. Former retail businesses, car dealerships, fire stations, and factories become venues for resident companies and rental spaces for itinerant companies. Space and budgets are always used "creatively"; many of these retrofit venues lack proper backstage space or adequate dressing rooms. Even if a company has the budget to fully cast *Much Ado About Nothing*, there might not be enough room either on or offstage to contain all the actors, let alone provide and store their costumes. Despite the physical and financial constraints, the artistic vision of these Chicago storefront theatres is boundless.

When challenged by space and budget, casting fewer actors for productions is a sensible solution for these companies. Lifeline Theatre, founded in 1982 in Chicago, focuses on bringing new works and adaptations to the stage. They adapt epic novels such as Tolkien's *The Two Towers*, Jane Austen's *Northanger Abbey*, and Alexandre Dumas *père*'s *The Three Musketeers* and perform them with ten actors, a costume budget of $2,000, and ambitious (some might say reckless) imagination. Actors cast in Lifeline productions are assigned to "tracks," which can include one to twenty different characters. For example, the actors playing the titular Musketeers play only Aramis, Porthos, Athos, and d'Artagnan. However, the actor playing Cardinal Richelieu also plays four other characters, including a soldier in service to the cardinal, a soldier in service to the king, and various ruffians for the Musketeers to dispatch.

Costume designer Rosemary Ingham likens designers to "crime scene detectives" searching for clues about characters, which become the basis for the costume designs.[1] Factoring in demands from countless sources, a costume designer fashions the external "body" of a character, something that requires an impressive understanding of costume history, literature, art history, theatre, clothing construction, anthropology, and human psychology. Ingham states that "designers have a special knowledge about the effects of design on human responses."[2] The costume designer curates the visual external body of the character while the actor gives life to its heart, mind, and the physical body in motion. Oskar Schlemmer notes, "The transformation of the human body, its metamorphosis, is made possible by the costume, the disguise."[3]

The actor is the owner-operator of the original human body that is to be transformed into the new character body. When the external physical costume change between characters is restricted, the actor might choose to push contrasting physical and vocal traits within a track to compensate. If there is no time to change costumes between Old Man #1 and the Innkeeper, then an actor might choose to give Old Man #1 a severe limp and the Innkeeper a working-class dialect. In the absence of a complete visual change of the actor's body through costume, the challenge of creating each new character body falls more heavily on the performer and the specificity of physical and vocal acting choices.

When costumes are not able to change completely to suit each character, then neutral garments flexible enough to work for all characters can be employed. Mirroring the Shakespearean unit set, the designer creates a neutral base costume shared by all the ensemble actors. Layering costume pieces and accessories can alter this "visual baseline": the base costume on ensemble actors can provide contrast to the lead characters. This concept works wonderfully in Paul Tazewell's designs for the musical *Hamilton*. The all-purpose uniforms of the chorus enable them to function as a cohesive visual unit and then nimbly transform into new characters with the addition of a military coat or an accent piece.

There are certainly instances when an ensemble actor playing multiple roles needs substantial costume changes rather than relying on small external alterations and actor virtuosity. There is no scientific way to measure what is enough when it comes to differentiating between these characters for the actor and audience. It becomes a "Goldilocks" problem: you won't know what is just right until you see it onstage in action. In addition, many variables completely external to the choices of the costume designer and the actor can actually dictate costume changes. If actors are blocked to never leave the stage, then changes need to happen in full view of the audience or not at all. Transitions between scenes might be impossibly short or the actor may be required to move props or scenery for the next scene. Limited backstage space or the distance to the dressing room can eat up the ten seconds the playwright so generously gave the actor to make a change. These are but a few of the factors impacting costume choices and that generally require a design strategy be simplified in order to maintain the flow of a play for successful storytelling.

In order to streamline the costume changes, the designer needs to discover what pieces are essential (if any) to a costume in order to clearly communicate a character. Aoife Monks describes costume as a "body that can be taken off."[4] When a costume change occurs onstage, the audience witnesses a character's visual body being shed, only for the neutral body of the actor to step into the new skin of another character. This can be a ritualized moment of physical transformation. Or, of course, an actor can make this shift without the benefit of any clothing. Jerzy Grotowski argued, "It was consummately theatrical for the actor to transform from type to type, character to character, silhouette to silhouette—while the audience watched—in a poor manner, using his own body and craft."[5] In the 2008 production of *Mojo Mickybo* at the Seanachai Irish Theatre of Chicago, actors Dan Waller and Robert Kauzlaric became an entire Belfast neighborhood without any alteration in their simple casual costume. Any change in the external "costume body" would have been an unnecessary intrusion of reality, derailing the enjoyment of actor virtuosity and storytelling in that production.

Monks observes that an "actor's body is a composite of many bodies."[6] The audience is aware of the actor's body and each subsequent character's body. However, there are often additional bodies seen by the audience member that are indirectly connected to the witnessed performance, which may not even be present on the stage. For example, they might be thinking of a previous viewing of the same play at another theatre or of a recent film adaptation. The actor onstage might remind them of a boss they dislike, or the character as presented might be in conflict with the vivid image they created in their mind when they read the original book or play. The multiplicity of composite bodies is heightened when the actor is playing several characters within a play. Marvin Carlson points out that the "recycled body of an actor, already a complex bearer of semiotic messages, will almost inevitably in a new role evoke the ghost or ghosts of previous roles, if they made any impression whatever on the audience."[7] The audience is aware that the actor's actual body remains constant despite the shifting skins of the external body. These skins do not exist in isolation; rather, each skin leaves its mark on the previous skin. Each character body exists in conversation with past and future bodies.

The ghostly residue of composite bodies is a special problem for celebrity actors onstage. When Daniel Radcliffe played Alan Strang in the 2008 production of *Equus*, it was hard for critics to forget his work playing young Harry Potter even though he was now all grown up and onstage doing confusing things with horses. Ben Brantley's review in the *New York Times* illustrates this point: "For Alan Strang is, in a sense, a tidy inversion of Harry Potter. Both come of age in a menacing, magical world where the prospect of being devoured by darkness is always imminent."[8] In a 2008 interview with *The Guardian*, Radcliffe stated, "[*Equus*] is a really intense, sexual and in some ways violent play, and some of the audience may be shocked. People may even possibly think that I shouldn't be doing it because of the Potter fans. But I think that would be a mistake. . . . The person at the center of all the attention should always be the one to lead where the attention goes."[9] The actor carefully chose this role as a decisive means to shed the "skin" of a much-loved character and also to announce his refusal to let that prior character define his future career.

This celebrity problem is experienced on a smaller scale in the ensemble acting companies of Chicago. The subscriber base of Lifeline Theatre takes great pleasure in seeing beloved company actors take on each new role. Their enjoyment in each new performance comes from seeing the familiar ensemble actor's body wearing new skins within a larger context of all the skins that the actor's body has previously worn. Monks states that "the actor's body accumulates its own history of meanings through its costuming," which is then "continually reformulated through costuming and through the reception of that costuming in a variety of roles."[10] Just as a unit set becomes a variety of locations that are altered by sound and lights, so too is the actor's body a host for a variety of identities.

The purposeful layering of character bodies on one actor's body can produce a beneficial meaning; however, this is not often a luxury afforded to many productions. Frequently the choice of actor for a character in a play like *The Three Musketeers* is not about who would play the part best but rather who is available, not during the initial casting process, but quite specifically whose body is not already in use onstage at that moment. The casting becomes a complicated flow chart of actor entrances and exits to be coordinated with the playwright, director, designers, and actors. With each character shift the audience is confronted by the mechanisms of theatre and is witness to an occurrence that is distinctly theatrical. In the best of circumstances, an interesting conversation can unfold between the actor's disparate characters. When the layering can be intentional, the results can be quite profound. In Shakespeare's Globe's 2015 traveling production of *King Lear*, Cordelia and the Fool were both played by Bethan Cullinane. Both characters' costumes kept the same color scheme, in part by repeating a simple yellow floral print dress as the base costume, with the Fool adding a red knit coxcomb hat, rust vest, and oversized trousers on top of base dress to alter the silhouette. As Cordelia, she added a rich brown and gold tapestry surcote over the dress. The shared costume body (the yellow floral dress) tied the two characters together visually while the story and each character's relationship to Lear bound them with thematic and emotional intent.

Cordelia and the Fool, through words and action onstage, provide the audience with plenty of information to understand their characters. The costume reinforces the text, and the shared costume body between Cordelia and the Fool adds additional meaning for the audience. Since costume is often the first way for the audience to view characters prior to the moment they speak and interact, it stands to reason that costume can also be the primary means to grasp intention when characters have little to no dialogue.

All characters onstage have some function, and the costume must serve and support that purpose. While directing the large cast of *Detective Story* at Strawdog Theatre in Chicago, Shade Murray described characters in terms of "sprinters and long distance runners."[11] Some characters make brief and explosive impacts on the story, while others build meaning slowly and steadily. When costuming characters, Rosemary Ingham suggests that "seeing the characters in terms of the jobs they perform allows designers to successfully create and manipulate the visual focus on the stage."[12] With "distance" characters, there is time to develop and reveal the identity through clothing in tandem with the actor's work. The "sprinter" characters, however, burst onto the scene and then take their leave; consequently, both actor and designer must rely heavily on clear visual cues to help the audience understand the purpose of a "sprinter" character.

Since the designer's work usually begins long before a cast is in place, preliminary costume choices can be very influential to the actor's subsequent process. Erika Fischer-Lichte affirms that the external appearance, or the costumed body, "provides the outline of an identity" that is then made "concrete" by the actions of the actor.[13] Here we see resonance in the phrase "getting into character." The costume becomes the physical representation of the character, a character body, that when put on becomes a tool for the actor to activate and achieve the character.

While these costume bodies are an important tool for actor character creation, there is a potential trap in giving performers more than is necessary to signal each new character. Roland Barthes discusses how a costume "must find that kind of rare equilibrium which permits it to help us read the theatrical act without encumbering it."[14] Making the actor who is playing ten characters change into and out of ten full costumes seems like the very definition of "encumberment." So how does the designer in this situation enable and enhance instead of clutter and burden?

When the character's costume body is unable to be a complete body, due to external constraints, then the designer and actor must distill the costume body down to essential pieces or signifiers. The obvious and, in fact, the original solution to the challenge of multiple characters played by a single actor is the mask. In Italian *commedia dell'arte*, a character was instantly recognizable by the mask and costume. Mask, as the signifier of a character, also conceals the identity of the wearer, allowing a single actor to easily play multiple roles.[15] However, in hiding the actor, the mask consequently creates an obstacle (in both the physical and emotional sense) between the performer and the audience, which is not ideal for most theatre performed today.

Costume pieces can also be a transformative tool similar to the mask. Eleanor Margolies observes that objects such as costumes can have a "fluid meaning potential" that is determined by how the actor uses the object.[16] A black mourning shawl worn tied around the waist by an actor onstage will not convey its originally intended purpose as an indicator of grief until it is worn about the head like a veil. That same mourning shawl could begin as a waist sash, then become a scarf, later be used as baby swaddling, and then a funereal shroud in the course of a performance. When the object finally appears as a mourning veil at the end of the play, each use of the object will have built upon the previous one, creating a composite of meanings. Like the ghostly residue of previous roles left on an actor, residual meaning forms around the costume piece. The audience will remember the previous uses and the manner in which the mourning shawl had its own character journey on a small scale. The audience's cultural understanding of a costume or object can also build meaning. As soon as a gun appears onstage, the audience will exist in a state of anticipation for when it will be fired. The audience, likewise, waits for capes to be swished, spurs to jingle-jangle, and buckles to be swashed.

A trademark costume piece or prop can be a clear indicator for the audience once the convention is established and used consistently. Signifier pieces are especially useful for character delineation. However, this technique can get gimmicky. If used without restraint, the results could be an entire play of stock characters wearing eye patches, peg legs, and pince nez. Effective costume signifiers should enhance understanding and reinforce what the audience needs to know about a character. A threadbare apron that is still carefully cleaned and pressed indicates the financial realities of a character but also speaks of a character's pride and determination despite her situation.

Color and distinct motifs can be clear signifiers to define relationships and distinguish one character from the next. If the overall costume palette is neutral, then a garment of strong color can be the indicator for the new character. In Lifeline Theatre's modernized production of *The Three Musketeers*, the Musketeers wore blue T-shirts imprinted with a fleur-de-lis design, while the King's Guard wore the same style of shirt in white and the Cardinal's Guard wore red. Changing T-shirts was simple for the ensemble actors to do very quickly and minimized confusion for the audience during frenetic battle scenes.

When there is a hierarchy of importance among the characters played by a single actor, the character with the greatest impact might demand the most "complete" look. In the *Three Musketeers*, the actor playing Cardinal Richelieu wore a red velvet robe with a black cassock adorned with a jeweled cross and zucchetto (a Catholic cardinal's skullcap). Beneath this complete character costume body was the neutral base costume of black military pants, T-shirt, and combat boots. The actor's other characters had simpler signifier pieces: a cardinal's guard in a red T-shirt, a bandit in a poncho and hat, and a spy in a hooded cloak. Once the audience was introduced to the cardinal in all his liturgical refinement, it was then understood that the actor was only the cardinal when in that particular costume body.

If there is not a clear hierarchy in an ensemble actor's character track, then it might be necessary to identify which of the characters are the most similar and therefore most in need of contrasting looks to make the change clear. In American Theatre Company's barebones production of *Oklahoma!*, every actor, including the leads, played multiple roles. Each character had a carefully curated "signature" piece(s). A problem arose when the actor playing Ali Hakim had to take a hasty exit after the auction and then his other character, Slim, had to give the very next line. For the bulk of the show, he had enough time to make a more complete change between the two very different characters, but not for this moment. The decision was made that the Ali Hakim costume could be less complete for this final scene since his character had been clearly established before this point in the play. All that the audience needed in order to understand that the actor who had just left the stage as one character and entered moments later as another was to trade Ali's bowler hat for Slim's cowboy hat. Additionally, the moment usually resulted in laughter from the audience delighting in a uniquely theatrical moment that reminded them that they needed to remain active participants in the construction of the world they watched onstage.

Using these methods can assist the director, designer, and actor in creating functional costumes for the ensemble actor that not only facilitate the flow of a production but also can build additional meaning. Since the costume is a character body created by the designer in tandem with the actor, stepping into that character body, as Monks describes, can be a "means for the actor to access the world of the performance."[17] When the character costume body is unable to be complete, signifier pieces can stand in to represent the full character body in order to allow for ease of transition between an actor's multiple characters. Further, these costume bodies create a composite body on the performer in which all accumulated bodies work in conversation with each other to build meaning for the audience. When using these concepts, casting a small ensemble of actors to create a multitude of characters can be an asset rather than a necessary evil for small producing theatres.

Notes

1. Rosemary Ingham, *From Page to Stage: How Theatre Designers Make Connections Between Scripts and Images* (Portsmouth, NH: Heinemann, 1999), 49.

2. Ibid., 147.

3. Oskar Schlemmer, "Man and Art Figure," in *Theatre and Performance De-*

sign: A Reader in Scenography, ed. Jane Collins and Andrew Nisbett (New York: Routledge, 2010), 270.

4. Aoife Monks, *The Actor in Costume* (New York: Palgrave Macmillan, 2010), 11.

5. Jerzy Grotowski, "Towards a Poor Theatre," in *Theatre and Performance Design: A Reader in Scenography*, ed. Jane Collins and Andrew Nisbett (New York: Routledge, 2010), 283–84.

6. Monks, *The Actor in Costume*, 20.

7. Marvin Carlson, *The Haunted Stage* (Ann Arbor: University of Michigan Press, 2001), 8.

8. Ben Brantley, "In the Darkness of the Stable," *New York Times*, September 25, 2008.

9. Craig McLean, "Dirty Harry," *The Guardian*, February 10, 2007, https://www.theguardian.com/film/2007/feb/11/harrypotter.

10. Monks, *The Actor in Costume*, 25.

11. Shade Murray, director of *Detective Story* (Strawdog Theatre), conversation with author in rehearsal, Oct. 2003.

12. Ingham, *From Page to Stage*, 77.

13. Erika Fischer-Lichte, *The Semiotics of Theater* (Bloomington: Indiana University Press, 1992), 91.

14. Roland Barthes, "The Diseases of Costume," in *Critical Essays* (Evanston, IL: Northwestern University Press, 1972), 49–50.

15. Fischer-Lichte, *The Semiotics of Theater*, 75.

16. Eleanor Margolies, "Were Those Boots Made Just for Walking? Shoes as Performing Objects in Everyday Life and in the Theatre," *Visual Communication* 2, no. 2 (2003): 180.

17. Monks, *The Actor in Costume*, 20.

Embracing the Chaos

Creating Costumes for Devised Work

Kyla Kazuschyk

T YPICALLY, CRUCIAL ASPECTS of successfully creating costume designs and producing realized versions of those designs for theatrical practice include in-depth script analysis, careful study of characters, and detailed planning of materials and labor budgets. However, when the costumer is tasked with designing and creating costumes for a project that begins with no script, no characters, and sometimes even an amorphous cast, the wisest course of action is to embrace the chaos. The term "devised theatre" is used to describe a number of different types of production processes. In traditional theatre, the process usually starts with a team of people assembling around a script that specifies the plot, setting, and characters of the piece. In devised theatre, the team assembles, yet they often have no written text to use as a blueprint to guide the production journey. In some cases of devised theatre, there is written text, yet that text does not specify which character says which line, or who the characters are, or where they are, or what they are doing.

Another facet of the growing world of devised theatre is site-specific immersive theatre. Companies like Punchdrunk, Dream Think Speak, Third Rail Projects, and Speakeasy Dollhouse are creating new theatrical forms, in which traditional processes of costume design and production need to adapt in order to be successful. For example, on Punchdrunk's production of Poe's short story "The Masque of the Red Death," the costume designer worked with the team to create the atmosphere and the experience:

> Combining the classic tales of Edgar Allan Poe with the buried Victorian origins of Battersea Old Town Hall, *The Masque Of The Red Death* lured audiences into a macabre world of mystery and the supernatural.

Exploring some of Poe's most disturbing themes and obsessions and populated by a large cast of bizarre characters, *The Masque Of The Red Death*
played for a 7-month sold out run and was seen by over 40,000 people.[1]

The process for creating the costumes for this large cast of bizarre characters began with a stockpile of researched, period-appropriate costume
pieces that were then fit to the actors. Performers were given costumes to
use in rehearsals; they then had the opportunity to improvise ideas about
how those costume pieces could express character before they went back
to the costume team to be adjusted and completed.[2] In a piece where the
characters are clearly described by the script, designers and actors do not
have the same amount of freedom to improvise and make adjustments
to whom the characters are.

It can be a challenge for the costume department to plan, organize,
and assemble items for performers to wear while the entire shape of the
piece is constantly changing. Clothing for the stage is inextricably linked
to the expression of character. Numerous sources offer guidance on how
to create costumes for characters already defined in a script, yet few resources are available to guide the theatre artist through the journey of
creating costumes as the characters are also being simultaneously created.

Two recent devised theatre projects serve as useful examples of how
to proceed with costuming for devised theatre. As costume designer,
cutter/draper, and costume shop manager for Sam Shepard and Joseph
Chaikin's *Savage/Love* and Caryl Churchill's *Love and Information*, I was
able to participate in all aspects of the theatrical costume process, from
inventing underlying meanings to ensuring that costume pieces appropriately fit the performers' bodies. Characters grew to shape the costumes,
and costumes influenced the establishment of characters. Instead of shaping characters around information given in a script, actors could mold
characters around the garments they wore.

The accepted design process for costuming follows seven basic steps:
commitment, analysis, research, incubation, selection, implementation,
and evaluation.[3] In traditional production processes, these steps are followed in mostly sequential order. In devised theatre, these steps need to
occur sometimes simultaneously and sometimes in a seemingly random
order, depending on the needs of the particular production. For designers
trained in the text-based method, shaking up the process can be fright-
ening. For actors and directors as well, beginning without a clear blueprint may feel scary. Chaos can seem threatening to a system that thrives
on order, though sometimes the strongest ideas emerge from this chaos.
When the needs of the costumes for the characters are not dictated by
an outside source, there exists the freedom for the costumes to be born
as the characters are born, to develop alongside the characters, and ulti-

mately to be more steeped in connection to the characters than costumes that are added on top of existing characters.

The "analysis" portion of the process involves studying and dissecting the text. In *The Magic Garment: Principles of Costume Design*, a text frequently utilized in courses teaching costume design, author and costumer Rebecca Cunningham suggests reading the script carefully multiple times, analyzing structure and style, and beginning to answer questions about the world and the characters, such as "How many characters are there? Are they male or female? What kind of characters are they? Main characters? Chorus members? Stock characters? . . . What specifics are known about each one?"[4] When I first approached both *Savage/Love* and *Love and Information*, I attempted to address these questions, and was completely unable to answer them. The texts for each of these pieces are nonlinear and non-narrative; they do not describe characters at all, or even specify which character will say which line. *Love and Information* contains 50 scenes, plus 20 additional optional scenes, with instructions from the author that state that the order of the scenes may be rearranged. *Savage/Love* is written more like poetry than like a script in which lines are assigned to individual characters. The lines may be broken up between people, or all spoken by one person. Neither text has any indication of how many people must be cast or how many characters there will be.

Another trusted resource for the creation of costumes is *The Costume Technician's Handbook*, by Rosemary Ingham and Liz Covey. I, and many other educators, use this as a textbook for costume construction classes. In it, Ingham and Covey outline the steps involved in creating a theatrical costume, describing twenty-six steps that follow examining the design sketch with the designer.[5] This process is built around the idea that by the time the designer has created that sketch, the director has signed off on the design and production may proceed, subject only to minor adjustments near the end of the process. In the world of devised theatre, this process must be almost entirely revised. As a designer, it is impossible to draw design sketches at the beginning of the process because there is not yet any content to inform what those sketches should be. The traditional process cannot be followed, and designers must be open to a roller-coaster of new experiences and ideas, instead of a tried and true set of questions that may be answered. The chaotic process of creating costumes for devised theatre involves visual communication early on, designer presence in rehearsal, and the ability to be extremely flexible while preplanning as much as possible.

Any time artists come together to collaborate and create theatre, whether they are working from a traditional script or on a devised piece, clarity in all forms of communication is extremely important. We must be as precise as possible with verbal communication, and we must understand that exact precision with verbal communication might actually never be possible. There is no way to really be sure through talking or writing that the images in your head are the same as the images in another person's head. This is why we must transition to visual communication early and often in the production process. When Shakespeare's Richard III says "My kingdom for a horse," the director might picture a healthy, noble, muscular steed. If the costume designer is reading that same line and envisioning a gnarly black skeleton of a horse, their perspectives on the world of the play will be vastly at odds. By sharing research images as they discuss the design concept for the show, they can ensure that the costumes reflect a coherent vision for the play. When showing research images, initial sketches, or color renderings to the team, the costume designer has an opportunity to shape the growth of the piece. Perhaps the director didn't initially imagine the world being created onstage to be a certain way, but when presented with compelling pictures, the direction of the piece could shift.

What I have found to be most effective in terms of visual communication is collaged research images. This collection of images could be photographs, paintings, objects, or digitally created images. They could be clippings from magazines or newspapers, printed photographs, or digital files stored on a computer. An advantage to collaged images is that they can be evocative, specific, and fairly easy to edit. A savvy costumer can start with a large number of images, and then distill that collection down to the most vital. As the shape of the production evolves, some images will stand out as more relevant to the production's theme, and others can be left behind.

The poetic text for *Savage/Love* does not denote specific characters or settings, yet it does invoke underlying themes of love, connection, euphoria, longing, heartbreak, and anguish. I began as a designer would in a traditional process, by finding images that visually represented my emotional response to the piece. In this case, the images were a mix of anatomical drawings of human hearts, photocopies of torn-up love letters, surrealist collages depicting flowers growing out of hearts, medical images of blood vessels and veins, horror-movie images of disembodied hearts dripping with blood, and cheery valentine-like candy hearts. These images represented the themes contained in the text. When designing for a scripted show with specified characters, the initial emotional response images often end up being reflected subtly in the color palette or texture of the finished costumes. When I showed these images to director/choreographer Nick Erickson, before rehearsals had started, he was so inspired by their evocative nature that together we brainstormed that the costumes could include more literal representations of these images. Nick's vision for the piece was that it would include a mixture of dance, aerial performance, live acting, and projected recordings, all coming together to express the ideas contained in the script as well as the performers' own views of love and loss. Initial rehearsals with the cast involved reading parts of the script and taking measurements, as well as discussing personal experiences and perspectives on love and relationships. While a costume designer is usually closely connected to actors through drawing pictures of them, planning garments for them to wear, and talking to them about their characters in fittings, it is unusual to be as intimately connected as this. Since characters do not exist before the costume designer is involved, the costume designer's input, in the form of ideas communicated through visual images, can influence who the characters become.

Near the beginning of the process for *Love and Information*, I tried to follow the standard method of script analysis that a costume designer practices. The second time I read the script, I began to discover the futility of trying to answer questions like "How many people are in this scene?" "Is the person speaking male or female?" and "Where does this conversation take place?" Because the script does not specify who speaks which line, it was impossible to create a typical scene and character breakdown. So, instead, I made a list of over one hundred evocative symbols and ideas contained in the text. This list included red flowers, small snails, celebrity couples, diseased chicken entrails, binary code sequences, microscopic images of heart and brain cells from people suffering from schizophrenia and Alzheimer's disease, Jackson Pollack paintings, roller coasters, and stars. I collected images of these things by doing an image search online. I printed all the images out and kept them in a folder so that I could bring them to design meetings and table rehearsals, to share them with the director and the performers. Having images printed and cut apart allows a costume designer to move things around, group things together, and easily remove images that emerge as less instrumental to the developing story.

I later learned that finding an answer to my first question ("How many people are in this scene?") was still important, as it was necessary to know who was onstage at any given time. The people onstage in each scene changed at every rehearsal up until opening night. Attending as many rehearsals as possible enabled me to keep a running list of who was onstage at any given time, and being prepared by having lots of garment options available at dress rehearsal allowed me to make changes as late as that. The second question I had tried to use as a distinguishing factor ("Is the person speaking male or female?") ended up being much less relevant. Distinctions of gender became far less important to this story than differences in age and class. Two women can make a connection to each other as easily as a woman and a man can, and likewise two men. The director decided that some of the scenes in the play should be told from the point of view of a child, hence the importance of the distinction of age. For scenes about missed connections and miscommunications spawning from imbalances of power, using clothes to show the distinction in class between people was more important than using clothes to express the gender with which those people identified. The question of place and setting was addressed in subsequent meetings with the director.

When I brought this first set of images to director Tara Ahmadinejad, she was particularly interested in the pictures of celebrity couples in various stages of connection and heartbreak. Specifically, the photographs of famous people in airports seemed to invoke this complex desire that so many of us have, to simultaneously revere celebrities while asserting that they are, as tabloid magazines put it, "just like us!" After our first meeting, I refined my research further in this direction, amassing copious photographs of celebrities in airports. This research influenced not only the look of the costumes: it actually shaped the setting of the whole show. The director saw that the duality of an airport as being a relatable site for both connections and misconnections helped to tell the story. So, while often it is the given environment that offers clues to the potential expression of the characters through costumes, on occasion it is the costumes that give clues as to who the characters can become and where the play can be set.

Often production and purchasing for a devised piece must begin before the cast is finalized. Such was the case on *Savage/Love*. Initially introduced as a summer abroad project, the cast for the piece was contingent on students who could go on the summer study abroad trip. Work on the piece would begin in Baton Rouge, Louisiana; it would then travel to France where additional cast members would join the production, and finally the piece would be performed at the Edinburgh International Fringe Festival. The initial cast was a list of students who had expressed interest in the project. Over the course of several months, some ensemble members dropped out and others joined. In a perfect world, I would have waited until the cast was completely finalized before starting to purchase, build, and fit costume pieces. However, in this instance, if I had waited, there would not have been enough time left to get anything done. I moved forward as early as possible by purchasing a variety of dyeable garments in a range of sizes. As performers came in for the first round of fittings, I fit the plain white garments to their bodies, and then later added dye and paint treatments to indicate character, as the characters and stories developed. This flexibility allowed the ensemble to continue to experiment with blocking throughout the rehearsal process. Characters who grew to be connected to each other had designs painted on their garments that connected together when they were blocked to stand together or embrace. Because I waited until later in the process to complete the dye and paint treatments, the ensemble was able to make changes that could later be enhanced by costume details. These details are what give audiences clues as to who the characters are.

Audiences interpret signals about a performer's character before the character even opens their mouth, based on what the performer is wearing. When an audience sees a figure dressed all in black, they might assume the person is a villain, or in mourning. People who study theatrical design are trained in this manner of interpretation, and even those who do not specialize in theatre often have some degree of culturally ingrained propensity to make assumptions about a person based on what that person is wearing. In one of the few existing sourcebooks on the topic, *Costume and Design for Devised and Physical Theatre*, author Tina Bicat attributes this to skills of imagination: "Audiences may not all be skilled at recognizing the finer points of cutting or costume history, but they understand the messages that design gives, and are particularly good at decoding costume. All children use the dressing up box to help their imaginative life, and the skills they develop so early still exist in adults, though they may not be conscious at the time that the same skill is used by the costume designer."[6] So, not unlike children playing dress-up, when we put a police officer's hat on an actor, the audience understands that that person is a police officer. Costumes can also more subtly signify underlying traits and attributes, indicating if a character is trustworthy or suspicious, old or young, and so on. As Rosemary Ingham notes, "An effective costume speaks to the audience's subconscious store of knowledge and experience, helping them to identify the individual characters even before they speak and if they are silent."[7] In *Love and Information*, the audience understood that the actors wearing red, white, and blue scarves, white shirts, navy blue suits, and gold wing pins were flight attendants, while the actors wearing grey coveralls and holding mops were janitors. Some costumes stand out by being spectacular; others help tell the story by being realistic.

Often the most effective costumes are the ones that do not stand out at all. I have worked on a number of contemporary shows, both devised and scripted, where I hear comments from audience members following the show, akin to "Well, you didn't have to do any work, right? It looked like the actors were just wearing their own clothes." In the moment, this can strike a costume designer or technician as an insulting dismissal of their time, talent, and effort. However, these sentiments can actually be viewed as high compliments. If the performers made the donning of costume garments appear so effortless and natural, the work of the costume crew has resulted in the creation of apparently authentic characters. This is true in both traditional and devised theatre, yet in devised theatre it takes much more energy to arrive at a set of realistic-looking costumes.

Rachel Sullivan, of the Honest Accomplice Theatre, addressed the puzzle of designing costumes for devised work by saying, "As a designer, you need a lot of adrenaline to work with a devising project."[8] This is because nothing is ever solid, things are always changing, and the entire process is chaotic. Perhaps this chaos and the mentality that adrenaline is imperative stem from the inherent goal of some forms of theatre to present questions and ideas rather than solutions. Live theatre has the power to incite ideas by presenting multiple points of view simultaneously. Audience members can see parts of themselves in different characters and are hence more inclined to think about different sides of the story than they might be if the story were just dictated to them from one perspective. Some works of theatre tell a story and tie the ending together neatly, delivering solutions that may not inspire further thought. Devised theatre almost always strives to offer questions rather than answers. Costumes can only stay in the questioning phase for so long, though; eventually some solid decisions must be made and costumes must be created. "You can whip together a scripted play in a couple weeks," Sullivan attests, but creating a new devised piece takes much longer, sometimes nine months or more.[9] In some forms of devised theatre, the process is actually of greater importance than the product. This emphasis on process allows designers to be more involved with the whole creation of meaning and the expression of the themes in the piece than there is space for in traditional theatre.

All theatre is collaborative art, and devised theatre could be explained as art that is ultra-collaborative. In an ideal world, a devised theatre company is formed as a sort of intentional community, members joining or being selected to join based on their particular skills, with the understanding that the work and the artists will grow together.[10] In reality, there are a number of possible variations on this model, particularly in regards to how costumes are designed and created.

The first set of possible variables involves how many people are contributing to the project. Many hands make light the work, yet make heavy the amount of necessary clear communication. Fewer hands means a heavier workload, but less need to spend time and energy sharing information. An advantage to my multifaceted position of costume designer, costume shop manager, and sole cutter/draper on both *Love and Information* and on *Savage/Love* was that I didn't have to communicate to any other people how I would like my designs to be executed. A disadvantage was that I had to execute everything.

The second set of possible variables surrounds the existence or non-existence of a script. Some works of devised theatre begin with a finalized script. Other forms bring a costumer into the process as the script is being developed. In some dance and movement pieces, there will never be a script. In other situations, there is a script, but the script does not specify characters and/or settings. This makes it difficult for a designer to follow the steps traditionally defined as necessary to design and construct costumes. Without a script that specifies how many characters there are, one cannot estimate how much of the budget needs to be spent on each character. Without descriptions of characters or information in the script that illustrates characters, one cannot formulate ideas of who the characters are and what they should wear. Without knowing the specific setting, a designer cannot begin to form ideas of what would be appropriate to wear in this setting. The collaborative team must invent a setting.

Such was the case in the two main examples cited here. *Savage/Love* is a series of poems by Sam Sheppard and Joseph Chaikin about love and loss and connection. This work became a multi-media, multi-disciplinary performance piece that evolved over the course of several months. *Love and Information* is a nonlinear collection of over fifty scenes about connections and missed connections in the modern world, written to be performed by an unspecified number of people, portraying an unspecified number of characters, in an unnamed setting. Over the eight-week production period within the academic calendar of Louisiana State University's 2016–2017 season, this production eventually became ten actors playing over one hundred different characters, in an airport. The nimble nature of a piece like this allows it to adjust to current events and bend to the perspectives that each individual contributor brings.

While strong research images can help to expand the visual or conceptual world of a devised piece, it is also vital for a costume designer to know the available resources well. As late as one week before dress rehearsal, seven out of the ten actors in *Love and Information* ended up playing flight attendants, in addition to the dozens of other characters they were already playing. Because I knew exactly where our navy blue suits and separates were in stock, I was able to pull them quickly. After brief fittings, I made the necessary alterations quickly as well. To complete the look, I ordered some plastic wing pins and red white and blue scarves online, which arrived in two days. Without being familiar with these resources, I would not have been able to accommodate the last minute additions of characters. In traditional theatre, there are still sometimes last-minute additions, but they happen on a much smaller scale than in devised theatre, and a costume designer has more time at the beginning of the process to make decisions and make plans.

Often, devised work can be a prime example of the "hurry up and wait" principle. While waiting for decisions to be made, a costume designer can be pulling multiple options, or at least becoming familiar with the options that are available, to be prepared to pounce on them when the time is right, that is, when the show is cast or when the characters are set. For *Love and Information*, I assembled what was essentially a closet of garments for each actor: a variety of pieces that fit the actor, could be coordinated and worn in a variety of ways, and could be worked into various scenes. Ordinarily, the costumes that an actor wears throughout the course of a show should reflect the arc that the character undergoes. In devised work, however, the through-line can be less of an arc and more of a zig-zag, with the interplay between one look and the next less related than they might be in more traditional productions. Preparing more options than you might eventually need sets you up for the future chaos of dress rehearsals, during which characters might be added in anywhere. Adding or subtracting layers like jackets and hats can very quickly shift a performer from one character to another. This zig-zagging character arc enhances a piece's ability to tell a story from multiple points of view. Characters that appear onstage for a short amount of time can represent different facets of a story or theme.

Part of embracing the chaos of devised work is being ready to let anything go. My initial color scheme idea for *Love and Information* was based on microscopic views of diseased heart and brain cells. As the piece developed, the director felt that a palette of "dusty neutrals" would be more appropriate for the world they were creating in rehearsals, so I shifted my key inspiration pictures to photographs of diseased chicken bodies (an image also referenced in the text). The beige, peach, and mauve tones combined with the tones of grey, black, white, and dusty green from other research images. Maintaining the somewhat scary view that nothing is precious leaves you open to new and bigger ideas. An initial idea a costume designer had independently may seem like the best possible solution to a problem, yet when thrown into the collaborative think tank of an ever-changing work of devised theatre, other collaborators might offer fragments of new ideas that coalesce to form something greater than any one of them imagined individually. Costumes are one piece of a larger puzzle that becomes the presented work.

The first dress rehearsal of one of the scenes from *Savage/Love* went exactly according to plan. The scene in question is about two people who pass each other every day at their mailboxes, each one hoping the other is noticing and sharing their longing. In the end, they do see each other and make a passionate connection. My research images included photographs of large-scale coordinating tattoos. The idea of tattoos ties into the theme of reckless passion that leads to lifelong scars. The piece was staged with the two people standing still on opposite sides of the stage, facing the audience, as dozens of other people ran around them in every direction. At the point where they began to connect, they faced each other and walked toward each other, eventually embracing. This staging was partially built around my idea for costumes that, on their own, looked like a random assortment of incomplete lines and partial shapes, yet when the two performers embraced, created an image in which the lines formed larger connected lines and recognizable shapes including geometric hearts. In other scenes, the performers appeared again, still covered in bold and incomplete lines, yet when surrounded by other people the connections remained incomplete. When the piece traveled to France for its next stage of devising, one of the performer's custom, hand-painted garments got lost. From the US, I advised my assistant to find him a plain white tank top and black yoga pants to wear. I was disappointed that some of the magic of my idea had been lost, but I had to make the most achievable choice with the given circumstances. The show was able to be presented and the story was still told, minus one of the costume details but plus the contribution of international performers.

In a typical design process, a costume designer might attend one or two rehearsals, usually included in the rehearsal schedule as a "designer run." This can help the designer to see the movement and blocking, entrances and exits, and the formation of characters. A character that may have seemed shy in the first reading of the script might appear sarcastic and outgoing onstage, as individual actors bring their own points of view to the formation of the character. In a devised process, it is imperative that a designer attend as many rehearsals as possible. Not only does this send the message that you are a team player who is invested in the whole project, it also begins to provide the answers to such questions as: Exactly how many people are in this scene? And are they playing specific characters? Do they need to be able to do cartwheels, back flips, or high kicks in this costume? Does the costume need to be specially fitted so that the performer may safely do tricks on aerial silks? On *Love and Information*, the number of people onstage in each scene continued to change up until opening night. At some points, the actors onstage had an integral part in the scene, while at other points the actors had the purpose of moving furniture to set up for the next scene, or comprising the background of a busy airport. In rehearsals, I was able to see their individual characters forming. Some characters ended up being very specific, like flight attendants, security guards, custodians, and children, though those distinctions were not all finalized until a few days before the show opened. In *Savage/Love*, some of the pieces involved performers standing or walking onstage, while others involved the aforementioned backflips, lifts, and incredible tricks on aerial silks. By attending rehearsals and watching the shows develop, I was able to fill in the blanks of the scene and character breakdown paperwork that I was initially unable to do. Seeing the actors' movements informed how stretchy or how loose fitting garments could be.

While working on *Love and Information*, I observed the director leading the performers through a number of warm-up exercises at the start of every rehearsal. I could see relationships and trust beginning to form between members of the ensemble. The purpose of such warm-up games is to hone the skills the performers need to be aware of themselves and each other during the working day.[11] This awareness shapes the characters and the ensemble. Individuals discover who they are in relation to each other. Because no single character exists on their own, it is helpful for a costume designer to see them all together, instead of only seeing them one by one as they come in for costume fittings. Being present at rehearsal shows the director and the actors that the costume designer is an active participant in the company. This makes it easier for them to trust the costume designer, to listen to ideas about costume, and to feel comfortable offering their own ideas.

A concrete strategy for success in creating costumes for devised work is to invite the performers in and really listen to them. Talk to them about what they do onstage and who their characters are becoming. Meet with them in advance of fittings if possible. Listen to them about what makes them feel confident and comfortable. Integrate at least some of their suggestions into the final looks. For both shows, I found it quite helpful to meet with the performers in the costume shop and take a few minutes to listen to their perspectives on the piece. For *Love and Information*, I prepared for fittings by making a list for each performer of what scenes I thought they were in and who I thought they were in those scenes. Before we even started trying on clothes, I went over the list with them and made changes as necessary. For example, "Are you the one who is keeping the secret? Who is the other person to you, a friend? A lover?" I scheduled forty-five-minute fittings so that we would have time to try on lots of different clothes and talk about what felt right, who they wanted to be, and who they believed they could be. It was a delight to see them visibly grow in confidence as they looked at themselves in the mirror, often crediting some detail as solidifying a certain character, as in: "Oh, he wears basketball shorts? I get it. I see who this guy is now." It was helpful to hear their input, such as, "I think this character is the type to wear sunglasses and a scarf in the airport." Because I had pulled a variety of options and because I knew exactly where in storage sunglasses were kept, I was able to provide the pieces to complete that character almost immediately. This flexibility and efficiency allows the costume designer to truly be a part of the process of adding meaning to characters through costumes.

In the *Savage/Love* fittings, I talked to the performers about what sort of movement they would do in the piece and had them try it out in the fitting room to make sure the costumes could accommodate it. Some of the aerialists had very specific preferences about how tight or loose their garments should be, and what parts of the body needed to be exposed or covered up. In these instances, it is important to defer to the performer's preference, so as to ensure their safety. A costume designer is intimately connected to actors, and can help them find the best possible wearable tools to tell the story.

Savage/Love ended up being an ensemble of performers in scenes that involved solos or group work. Each had one costume look, representing one character that moved through multiple scenes, sometimes connecting with others, sometimes not.

Love and Information became ten performers portraying over a hundred specific characters, some added as late in the game as final dress rehearsal. The day after the second dress rehearsal, the director approached me with concerns about the population of the airport that we had created. These concerns were not apparent when we had begun the process, in November 2016, but in late January 2017, airports were suddenly prominent in the news, as the new US president Donald Trump began proposing travel policies discriminating against people representing certain religions, ethnicities, and nationalities. Two days before opening is too late in the process to make significant changes to the set of any show, yet it is not too late to make adjustments to the costumes. After discussing possibilities with the director, I pulled a yarmulke, a kufi hat, and a scarf that could be worn as a hijab. I reviewed the script and what characters had been established, and determined which characters could be adjusted with the addition of these accessories. Costumes for devised work possess the power to change the piece as necessary, in a way that can quickly update the story being told, drawing it into an immediately wider and up-to-the-moment cultural context.

This connection to the world and to our humanity is inherent in all theatre, and especially powerful in devised theatre. Because the process for creating costumes for devised theatre goes hand-in-hand with the process of creating the work that will be presented, the costumes are deeply connected to the characters and to the stories they tell. Chaos is inescapable. Fear of chaos can prevent powerful stories from being told. Fear of the unknown can close the door to opportunity. As theatre practitioners, our job is to tell stories and to create magic. We are creating new worlds never before believed to be possible. Costumes are what create the fully fleshed out characters that inhabit those worlds. It is possible to tell stories and to forge connections. We learn who we are through relationship to each other.

Notes

1. "The Masque Of The Red Death," *Punchdrunk*, https://www.punchdrunk.org.uk/masque-of-the-red-death/, accessed June 25, 2017.

2. Tina Bicat, *Costume and Design for Devised and Physical Theatre* (Ramsbury, Marlborough: Crowood Press, 2012), 62–63.

3. J. Michael Gillette, *Theatrical Design and Production: An Introduction to Scene Design and Construction, Lighting, Sound, Costume, and Makeup* (New York: McGraw-Hill, 2000), 386. Other texts cover essentially the same ground, using slightly different terms or divisions. In *The Magic Garment* (Prospect Heights, IL: Waveland Press, 1989), Rebecca Cunningham lists these steps as reading and studying the play, collaboration between designers and directors, research, developing the costumes, unifying the whole, rendering the costume sketches, choosing fabrics for the costumes, and getting the show together. In *The Costume Designer's Handbook*, 2nd ed. (Portsmouth, NH: Heinemann Educational Books, 1983), Rosemary Ingham and Liz Covey list the following: the playscript, the production, costume research, preliminary sketching and color layout, final sketches, the pre-production period, and the production period.

4. Cunningham, *The Magic Garment*, 39.

5. Ingham and Covey, *The Costume Technician's Handbook*, 164–67.

6. Bicat, *Costume and Design*, 46.

7. Cunningham, *The Magic Garment*, 3.

8. Rachel Sullivan (director), in discussion with the author, March 2016.

9. Ibid.

10. Bicat, *Costume and Design*, 11.

11. Ibid., 28.

Dressing the Image

Costumes in Printed Theatrical Advertising

David S. Thompson

A N INFORMAL SURVEY of passages describing the duties of a costume designer and the functions of a given design in standard introductory theatre textbooks produces recognizable, even predictable, results. The textbooks speak of establishing time and place; indicating social status, occupation, or lifestyle; and reinforcing the mood or tone of the production. The costume design may, somewhat obviously, influence both movement and appearance of the actor. Costumes may be literal or figurative, stem from observation or offer a metaphorical approach. In short, the consulted texts provide a standard list of concepts related to textual analysis, artistic interpretation, theatrical collaboration, and the production of garments.[1]

While such a cursory literature review reveals many of the concepts that theatre professors might convey to their students, at least one concept emerges as conspicuous by its absence. Not one of the texts includes a mention of advertising or publicity.[2] Those who have worked with professional companies, or even larger university or community theatre operations, have probably created press releases that include photographs of actors in costume. It is not unheard of for larger commercial theatres to seek promotional value in eye-catching costumes. One example demonstrating the difficulty of such expectations involves a professor of costume design who worked for a regional theatre that typically wanted four or five costumes for a photo shoot scheduled shortly after the first rehearsal. The result necessitated a battle scene from *Henry V* or Peron in uniform alongside the iconic white gown from *Evita* built in five days or less.[3] Such an anecdote may produce groans or knowing nods from practitioners.[4] However, it nonetheless emphasizes a gap in the way we might otherwise consider the impact of costumes.

Since marketing campaigns often involve creating an image in the mind of the consumer, a potential audience member in the case of a theatrical production, the question becomes one of consistency. Is the image consistent with the product and is it accurate? Does the advertising image reflect the work of the designer or is the designer working along parallel, yet largely separate, lines? To explore these concepts, I consider some uses of costumes in printed theatrical advertising, eventually narrowing the focus to posters using photographs of costumes.[5] Finally, I wish to demonstrate some of the implications of costumes as marketing tools. As times, tastes, and techniques associated with such materials evolve, one may also detect evolutionary shifts in literal depictions and expectations of accuracy. Such shifts raise the question of whether audiences expect (or ever expected) truth in advertising. In turn, this analysis must adopt a bit of fluidity as the variations in posters, as well as the uses of costumes as images within them, require a somewhat variable and contingent engagement with the concept of accuracy.

Posters date to the Middle Ages, when standard bearers, known as vexillators, carried banners to announce guild performances or those of itinerant players. Town criers might announce details of the performance. For those who could read, brief handwritten descriptions were distributed and attached to posts in the area, leading to the use of the term "poster."[6] The first printed advertisement in English was created in 1477 by William Caxton, who is generally recognized as having introduced the printing press in England the previous year, and who would also become that country's first retailer of printed books.[7]

From those simple beginnings, posters would remain almost exclusively text-based for centuries, despite the fact that many could not read them.[8] Even a casual student of theatre history has likely seen examples such as handbills excitedly proclaiming a newly restaged Shakespearean performance or the poster listing upcoming attractions at Ford's Theatre including *Our American Cousin*, the latter image imbued with macabre foreboding for a performance destined for interruption by Abraham Lincoln's assassination. Regardless of the tone associated with these campaigns, the simplicity and convenience of moveable type, combined with the development of multiple typefaces, made the poster an obvious means for promoting a performance. Even after advances in printing technology, often resulting in greater ease in reproducing drawings and engravings alongside text, variations on text-based posters remained popular into the twentieth century, perhaps owing to habit as much as anything else.

By contrast, the English idiom that a picture is worth a thousand words, which has several possible origins spanning the nineteenth and early twentieth centuries, might explain the desire to include images in advertising during that same period. Although movable type in multiple typefaces was undoubtedly convenient during its time, a twenty-first century viewer cannot help but view such documents as having the opposite of their intended effect. Rather than the original intent of highlighting different names and titles, such posters and handbills now seem cluttered and resistant to quick reading.

Techniques for illustration, particularly woodcuts, were available, but were typically reserved for fine art prints and book frontispieces. Woodcuts became more popular during the mid-nineteenth century following the invention of electrotyping in 1838. This chemical process allowed for the duplication of objects with an irregular surface, including woodcuts. As such, a mass audience could have access to images from the era's popular melodramas, including the spectacle of *The Poor of New York*, the famous special effects from *The Corsican Brothers*, and the signature moment from *Under the Gaslight* (see figure 5.1).[9] In his book *Scenes from the Nineteenth-Century Stage in Advertising Woodcuts*, Stanley Appelbaum discusses the significance of this development: "For this era that was too early for on-stage photography (which began tentatively in 1883), these poster cuts show us how the productions looked. Nineteenth-century plays (especially melodramas) tended to be less talky than twentieth-century pieces and to rely much more heavily on the settings and on sensational effects."[10]

Unfortunately, Appelbaum's statement raises a pair of significant concerns, one practical and one theoretical.

Practically speaking, we cannot effectively verify that the woodcuts truly resemble an actual production. Since the images predate the advent of theatrical photography, authentication via some sort of eyewitness account would become necessary, a fraught concept in itself. It remains possible that the woodcut artist never saw a performance and only read a printed version of the script. The image might also have derived from a description provided by another person. Verifying such connections would require waiting for additional advances in technology that photography might provide. Of course, technological advances do not guarantee authenticity; a skeptic might opine that photographs can be manipulated and that financial gain (in this case, in the form of ticket sales) might provide motivation for illusions, if not delusions, of grandeur.

Theoretically speaking, even if one assumes that the woodcut is somehow a visually perfect representation, Appelbaum's assertion implies

Cut No. 175   UNDER THE GAS-LIGHT –1 sheet, 2 colors, $5 per 100.
Electrotypes of this Cut, in 2 colors, $12 ; in 1 color, $6.

Figure 5.1. An 1869 catalog listing for an electrotype of a woodcut depicting the locomotive scene from *Under the Gaslight* (J. H. Alexander, *Early American Theatrical Posters: Specimens of Show Painting in Miniature Form* [Hollywood, CA: Cherokee Books, n.d.], 61). [published 1869, public domain]

that only a single reading of the image exists. In the seminal essay "The Rhetoric of the Image," Roland Barthes offers a semiotic analysis of an advertisement for Panzani pasta, sauce, and Parmesan cheese, comprised of a photograph of the products with related grocery items and accompanying text. Barthes categorizes three classes of message: the linguistic message (text), the symbolic message (connotation), and the literal message (denotation). Within the second classification, Barthes notes at least four signs contributing to the symbolic message, but also notes that different individuals might detect a larger or smaller number. Such observations are far different from the how-the-production-looked assessment of nineteenth-century woodcuts. Since theatrical performance represents such a rich field of overlapping and interconnecting systems its analysis frequently becomes a semiotic field day, attaching multiple messages to the concept of a man tied to railroad tracks. Barthes suggests that drawing, which would include woodcuts, carries its own set of conventions, turning pen marks (or small cuts in this case) into their own codes. Barthes also positions photography as a potentially pure denotative form—a message without a code here in the present, but connecting us to something existing in the past. So, the shift from drawing and woodcuts to photography may well provide greater accuracy of imagery, even with a great many potential messages present.[11]

The latter part of the nineteenth century saw a series of advances in lithography allowing for more ambitious designs and more spectacular printed materials. Many of the posters and images created during the years leading to the turn of the twentieth century remain favorites today. This era—including as it does the Belle Époque and Gilded Age— is considered something of a golden age in poster art, encompassing advertising, propaganda, fine art, in a wide variety of expressions. Posters depicting performances in both the United States and France still carry appeal for collectors and undoubtedly enticed audiences of the period. Such temptations included advertisements for American burlesque and vaudeville performances as well as French cabaret, with artwork by Henri de Toulouse-Lautrec promoting the Moulin Rouge representing the epitome of the form. In such cases, images of costumed performers frequently supplied the means for conveying a lavish escapist fantasy. Given the exchange of creative energy between poster and performance, it is hardly surprising that theatre and its advertising would see increasingly more spectacular work.

For example, imagine a scene from *The Air Ship*. The poster for the entertainment depicts a fun-loving cast gliding through the skies in a delightfully idiosyncratic flying machine. Sadly, such images exist only in the imaginative world of advertising art. Although the poster indicates "an actual scene," there is no evidence that such a scene existed. The 1899 production, according to reviews, seems to have consisted of a series of sketches and random musical numbers, something more akin to vaudeville than a "musical farce comedy." The poster appears to be the product of the artist's imagination reacting to the title of the work (see figure 5.2).[12]

With the possibility of misrepresentation in mind, what should we consider when viewing twentieth- and twenty-first-century advertising, even when such materials include photographic evidence? In his book on posters, Max Gallo places the medium into historical context. He asserts, "The function of the poster today is to appeal to our subconscious feelings and our barely conscious needs and then channel them so that we do what the sponsor of the poster wants us to do. To discover not the literal but implicit intention of posters is to examine human behavior and history." He adds that "the poster is . . . a mirror that both reflects and distorts."[13] In his analysis of Broadway promotional materials Steven Suskin frames the exchange between seller and buyer by reminding us that theatrical art-

Figure 5.2. Poster for the 1899 production of *The Air Ship* (Michael Patrick Hearn, *The Art of the Broadway Poster* [New York: Ballantine, 1980], 37). [published 1899, public domain]

work represents what producers *intend* the show to be.[14] Of course, that may also suggest that producers intend prospective audiences to assume that resulting performances will meet both intentions and expectations.

Briefly returning to advertising imagery more generally, from the beginning of the twentieth century, many artists and critics have advocated for a purity of design. Often such purity comes from an approach borrowed from realism or naturalism. A simple reproduction of the article under consideration, rendered as clearly and beautifully as possible may transform it from a mere object "when it becomes as it were an advertising agent for the manufacturers."[15] The trick is to make an artistically pleasing photographic image of the product in isolation that does not descend into pedestrian catalogue illustration. One such success story may be found in the posters and advertising of Olivetti typewriters. Olivetti moved from elegant painted ads that seemed to tell a story (such as a woman looking joyfully at a new model) to equally simple photographs that let the product do the talking.[16] Similarly, fans of the television series *Mad Men* may recall one of several Volkswagen advertisements featuring the iconic vehicle photographed against a plain background. It accomplishes the same objectives as the Olivetti photo with the title of the accompanying text ("Lemon," in one example) providing an ironic counterpoint.

If promotional imagery contains the added touch of photographs of a performance, or elements of performance such as actors in costume, does theatre follow the advertising credo of letting the object speak for itself? Once again, does it do so effectively, accurately, or honestly?

It is not unusual to find company shots akin to family photos, as is the case with the 1916 poster for *The Blue Paradise* (see figure 5.3).[17] In this instance one might assume, with a level of confidence, that the costumes are accurate because the production had been running for some time. The show was transferring to the 44th Street Theatre from the Casino Theatre where, as the poster proclaims, it had played for an entire year. Yet records in the Internet Broadway Database indicate that the initial run was actually only ten months.[18] A skeptic with an eye for detail might wonder: if the producers, or their advertising representatives, felt free to exaggerate history, or seemingly change the duration of a year, might they also take liberties with the costume depiction? Viewing such a poster might also call into question any sense of accurately displaying the costume designer's work, since posed shots may provide a sense of garments on actors but not necessarily how they function to illuminate given circumstances within the production.

Similarly, anthologies of images akin to photo album pages often

Figure 5.3. Poster for the musical *The Blue Paradise* (1916) after its initial run (Maryan Chach, Reagan Fletcher, Mark E. Swartz, and Sylvia Wang, *The Shuberts Present: 100 Years of American Theater* [New York: Harry N. Abrams, 2001], 128). Courtesy of the Shubert Archive. [author claims fair use]

helped indicate the range of acts or scenes in a revue or spectacular. While the poster for the Shuberts' 1926 production of *Naughty Riquette* promised "a gay bouquet of singing and dancing buds," the visuals—a total of eight photographs arranged in rows, depicting subsets of the chorus and scenes among featured players—present the same sort of clutter that one might associate with a text-only flyer from the previous century. As such, the images of costumed actors on display might attract the attention of the curious, or its lack of focus might just as easily cause passersby to pass it by.[19] By contrast, the more restrained trio of images used on the poster for *Victoria Regina* of 1935 calls attention to the fact that the title role required Helen Hayes to play the monarch at several ages of her life. In this instance, selectively highlighting moments from the performance by placing the three photographs in the upper corners and across the bottom of the page serves to emphasize the arc of the action through costuming and staging imagery, while also retaining the practical advantage of reserving the center of the poster for the star's name above the title of the production.[20] The posters for both *Naughty Riquette* and *Victoria Regina* appear to employ costumes on actors portraying actual scenes (or poses) from the production being advertised. Each would appear to highlight accurate representations of the performance. Yet as advertising, the former poster falls short by forcing the viewer to assemble a coherent whole from the clutter, while the latter offers a sense of the celebrated aspects of the show. Just as a costume designer must collaborate with fellow theatre artists to ensure that garments enhance actors and coordinate design elements, a similar collaboration must occur with publicists in order to produce effective promotional materials that serve all parties.

Of course, selling a performance often involves selling the performers to the public. Steven Suskin asserts that photos of stars offer a selling point—something tangible for consumers to consider—even if they have no idea what the show is about. Stars of the past such as Katharine Hepburn, Gertrude Lawrence, and Ethel Waters, through more recent performers such as Cherry Jones and Idina Menzel, have appeared in posters for their productions. However, in each era the use of stars can assist in an accurate portrayal of the production or obscure it entirely. In the 1950 production of *As You Like It* that played in both New York and Los Angeles, Hepburn appears on posters as Rosalind, dressed as her alter ego Ganymede, contemplatively reclining in a wooden glen. Taken as a whole, the image serves to remind the viewer of the drag plot associated with the journey to the Forest of Arden. The details, a clear view of Hepburn's face and the fact that she is wearing tights, highlight the star power of a famous visage as well as her equally famous athletic physique.[21] Materials for *If/Then* run a range from a painterly drawing (nearly part of a storyboard in its effect) featuring Idina Menzel center and the cast in the background, to a solo photo of Menzel striking a pose during a song's climax, to a poster featuring photos of the cast, including two versions of Menzel in the foreground in two different costumes from the production. While each of these may resonate with various patrons, it is the final version that most reflects the key theme of duality, of choices and change within the musical, but it is also one that, short of cloning, is impossible to stage.[22] In the Broadway production of *Doubt*, Cherry Jones as Sister Aloysius wears the habit and bonnet associated with her order for nearly the entire production, but the poster opts for a variation on the costume in emphasis of a clearly rendered facial expression.[23] In the Boston tryout for *Lady in the Dark*, a circular headshot of Gertrude Lawrence appeared on the poster, not unlike standard photos used in ads for hundreds of summer stock productions through the years; the Broadway production featured a full-length photo of Lawrence in a striking black sequined gown, giving a hint of the glamorous surroundings of the musical.[24]

Stars may be used to become part of the imagery of the production, as with the 1997 revival of *The Diary of Anne Frank* starring Natalie Portman in her Broadway debut. Here the printed ad depicted Portman as the title character, dressed as a young woman in recognizably 1940s European attire, in a series of candid photographs arranged against diary pages. At least one of the photos recalls the style used for identification papers during the period.[25] Similarly, the simple image of Nathan Lane

and Matthew Broderick flanking a doorway—garbed in suits appropriate to a second-rate producer and a nebbishy accountant, respectively, in
1959—helped sell *The Producers* (not to mention the name Mel Brooks
and overwhelming word of mouth).[26] The star may also become the image. Few theatrical images are more iconic than Gwen Verdon striking a character pose in one of her most famous roles, in *Sweet Charity*.
As Charity offers an alluring wide-eyed gaze over her left shoulder, the
costume—a dress with a nearly impossibly high slit, a field of skin formed
by bare back and arms, and the requisite killer heels—supports the persona promoted by both character and performer. The image helps explain
why critic Walter Kerr gushed, "There are six things that will interest you
in *Sweet Charity*, the dances, the scenery, the songs, Gwen Verdon, Gwen
Verdon, and Gwen Verdon."[27]

Historically, printed ads featuring photos of actual scenes from productions seem far less common than posed photos or other graphic imagery.
Vincent Price in *Angel Street* may carry sufficient star power and there
is certainly an indication of the strained relationship on display. Price
as Mr. Manningham lounges imperiously in an elegant smoking jacket,
waistcoat, high collar and cravat, absorbed in his reading, indifferent to
the attention of Mrs. Manningham, portrayed by Judith Evelyn (see figure 5.4).[28] Would such an image pique audience interest in the thriller? Is
this a strong enough icon for sales purposes? Either it was, or the word of
mouth carried the day since the original production ran for three years.[29]

Arguably one of the most successful uses of costumes in a poster is also
one of the most accurate. After *A Chorus Line* won the Tony Award for
Best Musical in 1976, new window cards for the show began appearing
around New York. The top of the poster shines with the illuminated marquee of the Shubert Theatre, bearing the title of the show, while below it
a scrolling light display, paused conveniently, reads "BEST MUSICAL."
In the lower half of the card the cast assumes the roles they have longed
for as members of the most stunning chorus imaginable. The costumes
are a riot in shades of gold and its complements. Men wear gold lamé
tuxedos and bow ties with coordinating vests over white formal shirts.
Women wear gold tights and long-sleeved gold brocade leotards beneath
vests of gold and white stripes and bow ties that match the menswear.
The darkened background of the image evokes both the night sky surrounding the Shubert Theatre marquee and black drapes surrounding a
performance space. The costumes become a uniform, signifying solidarity
and belonging, as well as a reward for the countless hours spent wearing
mismatched togs in dingy rehearsal halls. This chorus has survived tales
of professional disappointment and personal tragedy in hopes of a moment just like this. Whether you know nothing about *A Chorus Line* or

SHEPARD TRAUBE
(in association with Alexander H. Cohen)
Presents

"ANGEL STREET"

by PATRICK HAMILTON
with

VINCENT   JUDITH   LEO G

PRICE   EVELYN   CARROLL

GOLDEN THEATRE

45th STREET WEST OF B'WAY., N. Y. C.   MATS. WED. & SAT.

Figure 5.4. Printed advertisement for the 1941 Broadway production of *Angel Street* (Maryan Chach, Reagan Fletcher, Mark E. Swartz, and Sylvia Wang, *The Shuberts Present: 100 Years of American Theater* [New York: Harry N. Abrams, 2001], 123). Courtesy of the Shubert Archive. [author claims fair use]

are devoted to the material or somewhere in between, evoking the glittering finale builds a sense of anticipation for the performance itself. The photo creates the image not only of what the producers *intended* to offer the audience, to return to Suskin's formulation, but also what the production had already delivered for most of the preceding year and would continue to provide for an additional fourteen years.[30]

Reviewing successful graphic design firms working in theatre today, one could do far worse than to look at the work of SpotCo. In just twenty years they have shifted from a kitchen-table upstart to a recognized leader. Their approach frequently combines strong graphics with design elements from the productions of their clients. In addition to the aforementioned publicity work for *The Diary of Anne Frank*, they are responsible for the downtown vibe of *Rent*'s poster, the Blue Note Records-inspired *Side Man* campaign, and the police blotter photos associated with publicity for the long-running revival of *Chicago*, complete with a hue known officially as "David Merrick red." By using the costumes of William Ivey Long in the individual photos on the *Chicago* poster, the team at SpotCo created an endlessly flexible collection of frames that they could mix and match for displays of every conceivable size, shape, and application, and which could be altered piecemeal should the producers wish to highlight new faces as cast changes occurred. However, yet again, *technically* those images are not from the Broadway production. The costumes used in the original series of photo shoots actually came from the City Center Encores production that had been staged during the previous year; other than a tweak or two for Roxie the designs are essentially the same. Plus, many of the images do not reflect scenes from the production or even locations within the theatre.[31] In fact, Long's studio confirms that, for a variety of reasons, he frequently must style posters or publicity shoots from existing items pulled from his studio collection.[32] The situation is similar to both *The Blue Paradise*, mentioned earlier, and *Vanya and Sonia and Masha and Spike*, which played at Lincoln Center's Mitzi E. Newhouse Theatre before its Broadway run at the John Golden Theatre. The Broadway poster features the title in the upper portion of the frame and the title characters (arranged left to right with Kristine Nielsen as Sonia, David Hyde Pierce as Vanya, Sigourney Weaver as Masha, and Billy Magnussen as Spike) wearing outlandish costume party attire that figures within the plot. Earlier costumes were used and then transferred both to another production and its associated publicity.[33] Naturally, it makes sense that images of costumes provided prior to the opening of a show would not necessarily replicate the final product. Otherwise, costume designers would be working far in advance of publicists, not to mention other members of the production team.

Each of the productions cited in connection with SpotCo advertising campaigns would go on to achieve both critical and commercial success. (In the case of the *Chicago* revival, that success continues.) However, each of these uses of costume veers markedly from the overtly literal notion that Stanley Appelbaum ascribes to nineteenth-century woodcuts. The woodcuts may tell us "how the productions looked," but only as filtered through the interpretive impression of the artist or printer. It is here that advertising differs from archiving. A record of an event, whether photographic or otherwise, might attempt to capture detail for the information of others. By contrast, selling the event depends upon creating an impression, attracting audiences by suggesting what the production's creators intend it to be, to reiterate Steven Suskin's assertion. In fact, the intent here may relate more to mood and tone as audiences may not necessarily see a poster image during a performance, but may more likely react to a performance in a way that relates to the reaction to the poster.

So, do we really expect literal and accurate representation in printed advertising? Did we ever? Did circus and carnival audiences ever truly expect to view tortoises the size of elephants and elephants the size of buildings as depicted in posters? Probably not. Just as advertisers tout products as "new and improved" or "the best" in a way that consumers accept as harmless hyperbole, promoting theatrical performances also trades in inflated impressions. However, in a busy society impressions must strike quickly; few of us have the time to read text-heavy ads or analyze images in detail.

Even after surveying examples from a variety of advertising approaches, finding distinct trends apart from those associated with more generalized directions of public taste and stylistic vogues remains difficult. For those who design and execute costumes (not to mention those who train costumers), an awareness of expectations not always readily apparent in the job description, namely responsibilities beyond the garments themselves, becomes critical when costumes are used to promote the production. More generally, theatre artists create images. Audiences respond to compelling imagery. And if the productions of *Sweet Charity*, *Rent*, *A Chorus Line*, and *Chicago* offer examples, audiences reward those who create compelling imagery. Whether producers and publicists promote theatrical creations literally or figuratively, using the work onstage provides the best guide. Costumes may occupy a place in creating imagery in posters and other marketing. While such usage may still follow a literal replication of performance moments, it seems increasingly more likely, and increasingly clearer, that they often assume figurative roles. Even photographically accurate depictions of costumes may become but an element in a larger, more metaphorical evocation of a production, but they function best in advertising when they emulate their function onstage, namely, to augment plot and character by evoking time, place, mood and tone.

Notes

1. Milly S. Barranger, *Theatre: A Way of Seeing*, 5th instructor's ed. (Belmont, CA: Wadsworth, 2002), 247–57; Oscar G. Brockett and Robert J. Ball, *The Essential Theatre*, 8th instructor's ed. (Belmont, CA: Wadsworth, 2004), 383–404; Kenneth M. Cameron and Patti P. Gillespie, *The Enjoyment of Theatre*, 5th ed. (Boston: Allyn and Bacon, 2000), 186–87, 196–98, 202–3; Edwin Wilson and Alvin Goldfarb, *Theater: The Lively Art*, 6th ed. (Boston: McGraw-Hill, 2008), 183–91.

2. I should emphasize that my consultation of texts merely serves as an indicator for purposes of demonstration. Speaking of costumes and costume designs in conjunction with public relations materials is not the norm for introductory texts. Far too many texts exist to guarantee that my observation applies universally. Indeed, such a passage may well be included in a text I have not consulted.

3. Marianne Custer, email message to author, November 16, 2016.

4. I first presented a preliminary version of this article at Theatre Symposium 26 on April 7, 2017, at Agnes Scott College in Decatur, Georgia. Since then, several costume designers and technicians have shared similar anecdotes from their own careers. Among them, I am most grateful to the editor of this volume, Sarah McCarroll, for confirming that such practices are quite common, or at least far from rare.

5. I use the word "poster" as an umbrella term due to its flexibility, although I am well aware that printers and publicists will differentiate among posters, billboards, three-sheets, lobby cards, window cards, heralds, and handbills.

6. "Theatre Posters," Victoria and Albert Museum, http://www.vam.ac.uk/content/articles/t/theatre-posters/, accessed April 5, 2017.

7. John Barnicoat, *A Concise History of the Posters: 1870–1970* (New York: Harry N. Abrams, 1972), 8.

8. Wendy Nelson-Cave, *Broadway Theatre Posters* (New York: Smithmark, 1993), 20.

9. J. H. Alexander, *Early American Theatrical Posters: Specimens of Show Painting in Miniature Form* (Hollywood, CA: Cherokee Books, n.d.), 61.

10. Stanley Appelbaum, *Scenes from the Nineteenth-Century Stage in Advertising Woodcuts* (New York: Dover Publications, 1977), ix. Dating the tentative beginnings of stage photography to 1883 references another work in which the same author analyzes images from the collection of the Museum of the City of New York wherein the earliest dated photograph corresponds to that year. See Stanley Appelbaum, *The New York Stage: Famous Productions in Photographs: 148 photos, 1883–1939, from the Theatre and Music Collection of the Museum of the City of New York* (New York: Dover Publications, 1976).

11. Roland Barthes, "The Rhetoric of the Image," *Image—Music—Text*, trans. Stephen Heath (New York: Hill and Wang, 1977), 32–51; Hugh NLN, "The

Rhetoric of the Image—Roland Barthes (1964)," Traces of the Real, https://tracesofthereal.com/2009/12/21/the-rhetoric-of-the-image-roland-barthes-1977/, accessed July 12, 2017.

12. Michael Patrick Hearn, *The Art of the Broadway Poster* (New York: Ballantine, 1980), 36–37.

13. Max Gallo, *The Poster in History*, trans. Alfred and Bruni Mayor (New York: American Heritage, 1974), 10, 12.

14. Steven Suskin, *A Must See!: Brilliant Broadway Artwork* (San Francisco: Chronicle Books, 2004), 7.

15. Barnicoat, *A Concise History*, 148.

16. Ibid., 147–48, 119, 129. For those unfamiliar with these typewriters or the associated marketing, an internet image search for "Olivetti posters" will yield an array spanning most of the product history.

17. Maryan Chach, Reagan Fletcher, Mark E. Swartz, and Sylvia Wang, *The Shuberts Present: 100 Years of American Theater* (New York: Harry N. Abrams, 2001), 128.

18. "The Blue Paradise," Internet Broadway Database, https://www.ibdb.com/broadway-production/the-blue-paradise-7048, accessed April 6, 2017.

19. Chach et al., *The Shuberts Present*, 132.

20. Ibid., 53.

21. Suskin, *A Must See!*, 86.

22. If/Then National Tour, https://www.facebook.com/pg/ifthenmusical/photos/?ref=page_internal, accessed July 9, 2017.

23. Anne Nicholson Webber, "Cherry Jones Talks with Theatre in Chicago," *Theatre in Chicago*, https://www.theatreinchicago.com/news.php?articleID=193, accessed December 1, 2017.

24. Suskin, *A Must See!*, 21, 59.

25. Drew Hodges, *On Broadway: From Rent to Revolution* (New York: Rizzoli, 2016), 27.

26. Mel Brooks and Tom Meehan, *The Producers: The Book, Lyrics, and Story behind the Biggest Hit in Broadway History!: How We Did It* (New York: Roundtable, 2001), cover photograph.

27. Suskin, *A Must See!*, 37.

28. Chach et al., *The Shuberts Present*, 123.

29. "Angel Street," Internet Broadway Database, https://www.ibdb.com/broadway-show/angel-street-1587, accessed April 6, 2017.

30. Chach et al., *The Shuberts Present*, 96. The poster described here has remained so iconic that an internet image search using the term "A Chorus Line poster" reveals that framed copies are available from several online retailers, including Wal-Mart. The New York Public Library manages copyrights for Martha Swope, whose production photograph provides a clear inspiration for the advertisement. Billy Rose Theatre Division, the New York Public Library. "Chorus in the stage production A Chorus Line," New York Public Library Digital Collections, http://digitalcollections.nypl.org/items/8917aed0-ae19-0131-c06e-58d385a7bbd0, accessed July 7, 2017.

31. Hodges, *On Broadway*, 23. In addition to the materials Hodges features in his volume, an internet image search using the term "Chicago Broadway poster" provides a sampling of the graphic variations employed for the production publicity.

32. William Ivey Long Design, email message to author, December 5, 2016.

33. Hodges, *On Broadway*, 185.

Costuming the Audience

Gentility, Consumption, and the Lady's Theatre Hat in Gilded Age America

Leah Lowe

THROUGHOUT AMERICA'S Gilded Age (approximately 1870–1900), the fashionable woman's hat, "this large umbrageous, befeathered or befangled fixture,"[1] was recognized as a commonplace nuisance in the theatres of the country's urban centers. These tall and often ornate hats blocked the view of the stage for those seated behind them and posed vexing problems for theatre managers, theatre critics, and etiquette experts as well as for spectators. In 1897, for instance, a performance of *The Girl From Paris* at New York's Herald Square Theatre was disrupted when a young lady's hat, "a most wonderful creation of the milliner's art, broad of brim, tall of crown, and with what looked like the entire plucking of an ostrich farm surrounding it," obscured the sight of the stage for two men seated behind her. After hearing them make "most discourteous and insulting remarks," Miss Dorothy Upshur "got mad and made up her mind to keep it on in spite of them." Her male companion, a Mr. C. A. Ledyard, was drawn into the conflict and a "wordy warfare" ensued. Ultimately Miss Upshur was forced to leave the theatre with Mr. Ledyard in tow to keep him from "mixing up with the two men who seemed to be quite as willing as he was for a rumpus." While Miss Upshur was embarrassed and vowed never again to wear a tall hat to the theatre, the account of the incident in the *New York Times* reports that the two men "had the sympathy of the audience, for there was a very perceptible ripple of applause when the lady and her escort left the theatre."[2]

Making its appearance at a time in which an ethic of middle-class respectability was being supplanted by a "culture of consumerism,"[3] the lady's theatre hat, I argue, situated its wearer in the midst of a dynamic and transformative social context. Like a costume designed for the stage, the theatre hat was "read" by others for clues concerning its wearer's class status and character. It signified equivocally, suggesting gaucheness and lack of consideration on one hand, and stylishness and sophistication on the other, thus revealing a central tension that confronted middle-class women of the era. Like scholar Richard Butsch, who tracks the increasing feminization of American theatre audiences through the course of the nineteenth century, I am interested in the relationship between "two cultural formations, respectability and consumption, that seemed to be opposites."[4] While Butsch tracks the shifting relationship between these aspects of culture over a hundred years, I am interested in how this societal change was represented to and by those navigating it as it was occurring. Examining the cultural context surrounding the theatre hat and the public dialogue it sparked in newspapers, magazines, and conduct manuals provides a close-up view of a fluid culture in which conflicting and contradictory social pressures competed for dominance.

Chief among the cultural forces at play in the theatre hat debates were those of respectability or gentility, behavioral codes that took hold among the white middle and upper classes in early and mid-nineteenth-century America. As "the forces of immigration, industrialization, corporatization, urbanization, mechanization, and a revolution in transportation" transformed the country during the Gilded Age, the population of cities swelled rapidly.[5] Cultural historians such as John Kasson and Karen Halttunen have argued that as class stratification intensified within the shifting society, middle- and upper-class citizens internalized complex rules of etiquette that distinguished them from the less fortunate.[6] The ethos of respectability posited that mastery of etiquette, the specific behavioral rules that governed all manner of social interactions from weddings and funerals to chance encounters between strangers on city streets, enabled these privileged citizens to demonstrate their class status and be recognized by their peers in a cultural context in which many traditional signs of class identification had been obliterated by rapid social change.

Idealized codes of respectable behavior were formalized and propagated through inexpensive conduct manuals and advice literature throughout the nineteenth century. These ubiquitous print materials guided readers through numerous social situations by spelling out the appropriate behavior required of them. Their ready availability acknowledged the economic fluidity of the era by providing a path for those aspiring to move up the class ladder. Women, in particular, were charged with upholding genteel standards and through their commitment to them, with inspiring positive social change. "It is the duty of American

women," argued John Young, author of *Our Deportment* (1882), "to ex-
ercise their influence from so high a standard of morals that the tendency
of society will continually be upwards."[7] By the late nineteenth century,
as women's presence and participation in public arenas such as the theatre had become widely accepted, etiquette experts adapted standardized particulars of behavior to cover situations that were scarcely imaginable in the early 1800s.

Conduct manuals and advice literature of the era insisted that good
manners, based on reciprocal consideration for one's peers and often explicitly linked to Protestant interpretations of the biblical Golden Rule,
were crucial to successfully navigating an evolving culture. They are described, for instance, as "the machinery of society" in an 1892 volume.[8]
One published in 1882 asserts that rules of etiquette "are to society what
our laws are to the people as a political body."[9] Advice literature emphasized the democratic nature of American society and maintained
that manners could be acquired through practice with such counsel as
"Society has its grammar as a language has, and that language may be
learned."[10] It made clear that a failure to abide by the laws of genteel
behavior had profound consequences: "To disregard them will give rise
to constant misunderstandings, engender ill-will, and beget bad manners and bad morals."[11] Given the variety of situations that a respectable
woman might encounter in the burgeoning Gilded Age city, however,
the niceties of reciprocity did not always provide solutions to social conflicts, as this *New York Times* article from 1896 concerning theatre hats
indicates: "It is not at all uncommon for the wearer of even a moderately
large hat to turn to the occupants of the seat behind to ask if her hat
is in the way. The one objection to this is that the courtesy of the request
inspires the person questioned to an equal courtesy, and an untruthful
answer that the head-covering under consideration will be, if anything,
an addition to the outlook upon the stage."[12] Despite such gentle satire,
advice literature insisted that the ideal middle class woman was one who
displayed concern for the comfort of others and adhered to the prescribed
standards of behavior appropriate to her position at all times.

While etiquette books and advice columns held up the ideal woman as
an exemplar of sensitivity and consideration, real women were subject to
other cultural pressures. After the Civil War, developments in manufac-
turing and transportation revolutionized commerce as goods once produced in the home became available for purchase. By the 1870s, as wom-
en's traditional roles expanded to include shopping for their homes and
families, department stores had begun to address women as economic actors. Cultural historian William Leach argues that the late nineteenth-
century department store "pictured the desirable as did no other contem-

porary institution." Showcasing goods "as if they were not stores at all but theatrical havens, imaginative mediums," the department store enticed women to buy through secular appeals to sensual pleasure. In his study of early department stores, Leach identifies a cultural shift toward consumerism that transformed women's behavior through "the opportunities and imaginative culture" they offered.[13] Historian Kathy Peiss concurs and observes: "Shopping may have been understood by husbands as merely an extension of women's domestic sphere, but the experience itself, as constructed by retailers and female shoppers, may well have destabilized this notion. This largely female public culture admitted desire, emotion, sensuality, and fantasy as legitimate and motivating aspects of identity."[14] Peiss identifies the department store along with the restaurant, vaudeville, the theatre, and "fashionable promenades" among the "public pleasures" newly available to women in late nineteenth-century urban America.[15]

Just as advice literature offered readers instruction in the acquisition of middle-class gentility, the department store offered those who wandered its aisles an alternative curriculum. Historian Elaine Abelson calls the department store "an ideal realization of a materialistic age" and suggests that it was "infused with images and symbols of the aspiring middle class." She argues that artful arrangements of goods enticed desire and that "middle class shoppers were expected to want, if not to purchase, what was visibly displayed all around them."[16] A *New York Times* article from 1903 describes the inculcation of desire as education as it imagines a conversation between a department store clerk and its author. Many women, the clerk remarks, "have learned everything they know about good clothes and polite society in general in a department store." When asked if customers really come to the store in order to learn, the clerk replies: "Some of them do. That woman that you see standing over there by the sitting room door is a student. We call women of her type students because they dawdle around in the department stores acquiring knowledge. Just now the fur department is their happy hunting ground. They don't want to buy, neither are they especially anxious to know the prices; but they do want to be able to distinguish one kind of fur from another. . . . In other seasons the students study laces, and although they may never wear a piece that cost more than 15 cents a yard their department store experience has taught them to know the real thing when they see it."[17] Like sumptuous department store displays, illustrated women's fashion magazines such as *Godey's Ladies Book* and *Harper's Bazaar* contributed to the edification of the female consumer by "educating the eye, channeling desires, and creating an identification between representation and viewer."[18] While conduct manuals taught women to observe rigid behavioral codes, consumer culture instructed them to satisfy their longings for material goods.

Connections between early consumerism, represented by the department store, and the theatre were strong. In nineteenth-century New York City, for instance, department stores, cafes, restaurants, and theatres existed in close proximity along Broadway and the shopping district known as "the Ladies' Mile." Theatre historian Marla Schweitzer notes that these businesses "fostered strong cross-industry ties" in their pursuit of female customers. Wednesday afternoon matinees, for instance, regularly offered by the 1850s, enabled women to shop and see a performance in a single outing. Schweitzer argues that nineteenth-century theatre managers and department store owners "worked hard to feminize consumption and to choreograph feminine movement between their establishments."[19] Nor was the connection between stores and the theatre just one of proximity. In *When Broadway Was the Runway*, her study of the relationship between the commercial theatre and the fashion industry in the early twentieth century, Schweitzer asserts that the theatre introduced women to new trends in fashion through the costumes worn by popular actresses. "As the most dominant, widespread entertainment forms in the United States, with a demographic and geographic reach much greater than that of the individual department store," she observes, "the legitimate theater and vaudeville, its popular counterpart, were well positioned to shape modern American consumer culture, especially tastes in fashion."[20] Like women's magazines and department store windows, the theatre itself played a role in cultivating feminine desire for stylish material goods.

Among the consumer goods featured in fashion magazines and department store displays were newly available ready-made clothes and accessories. While the hats and bonnets of the early 1870s were "little more than decorative headdresses," by 1875 they "grew impressive in shape and decoration" to accommodate elaborate hairstyles.[21] Fashionable hats of the 1880s, historian Joel Shrock reports, "were heavily decorated with ribbons, flowers, plumes, and even small stuffed birds." Hat trimmings "tended to be in brilliant blazing colors like bronze, gold, garnet, and peacock blue."[22] In contrast to the traditional bonnets of the mid-nineteenth century that were tied under the chin, these large hats, often peaked in a triangular shape, were secured to the head with long decorated hat pins, making them more difficult to remove. Late nineteenth-century illustrated fashion magazines like *Harper's Bazaar* are replete with pictures of large hats designed for street wear, but even when the head covering itself was small, its embellishments often proved obtrusive in the theatre. "In point of fact, one of the most intolerable nuisances is the small bonnet with a great fan of aigrettes at one side," a *New York Times* article reported in 1896. "The success with which these feathery points can obscure an entire stage from its spectators is only equaled by their maddening effect on the piece of mind of their victims."[23] Fashion magazines and newspapers reported on millinery with great enthusiasm, emphasizing the abundant variety of shapes, fabrics, and embellishments used in hat construction in their accounts. The acquisition of such hats, like that of other fashionable objects, is depicted with an excitement designed to foster desire.

In public and on city streets, hats were a compulsory aspect of middle- and upper-class feminine attire. Given their necessity and their frequently elaborate trimming, they often functioned as a kind of flash point that demonstrated tensions between appropriate feminine modesty and excessive feminine extravagance. Women's hats were discussed heatedly in multiple public forums. In 1897, for instance, the *New York Times* reported on a well-attended meeting of the Audubon Society at the American Museum of Natural History convened to discuss "why it was wrong for women to eke out their personal beauty by dint of dead birds, or parts of birds, worn in their hats and bonnets."[24] In a letter to *The Christian Union* in 1887, the famous clergyman Henry Ward Beecher reported that he was asked to weigh in on the subject of women's hats, although he neatly avoided offending anyone by declining to discuss it in any depth.[25] Even William Dean Howells, "The Dean of American Letters" himself, opined in the pages of *Harper's Weekly* that the wearer of the theatre hat was "a person of rather a simple mind, who thinks that to see her empty little head crowned with a confection of felt, ribbons, and feathers . . . will be a consolation to those it keeps from seeing the play."[26] These public discussions and press accounts of women's hats provided opportunities to air anxieties about shifting cultural values and gender norms.

As respectable women attended the theatre in increasing numbers during the late nineteenth century, etiquette books and newspaper advice columns began to instruct them in spectatorship. The proper behavior proscribed in the advice literature of the Gilded Age for attendance at the theatre would seem familiar to twenty-first century audiences for the most part. Theatregoers were encouraged to arrive on time, be quiet during the performance, and to refrain from rustling programs and passing bonbons up and down the aisle. There were, unsurprisingly, numerous rules that governed what respectable women could wear to the theatre. In general, "for the matinee, the costume required is like that which should be worn on the street or in a carriage."[27] While none of the advice literature recommends deliberately antagonizing those audience members who are seated behind by blocking their view with a large hat, such hats were a required part of street and promenade costumes. On this point, the advice literature became somewhat equivocal, because just as there were strict rules about being sensitive to the comfort of others at the theatre, there were equally strict rules about what could and could not be worn in the street or on streetcars. *Decorum*, a conduct manual written in 1883, notes, "In some cities it is customary to remove the bonnet in the theatre—a custom which is sanctioned by good sense and a consideration of those who sit behind, but which has not yet the authority of etiquette."[28] Many advice authors recommend a smaller bonnet or a "soft Alpine cap" that could be removed and held in one's lap during the performance.[29]

Despite the sensitivity to others recommended by the authors of advice literature and the apparent social acceptability of the smaller bonnet, the frequency with which the large theatre hat is mentioned in the popular press indicates that it remained a point of contention throughout the Gilded Age as cultural norms and values shifted. It was the subject of editorial cartoons, snide newspaper and magazine articles, and numerous letters to editors of the nation's newspapers. The tone of many of these public discussions, often both jocular and critical, is captured in "The New Theatre Hat," an 1898 article. At a matinee, the *New York Times* reports, two men were seated behind two women wearing "gems of millinery striking enough to move women novelists to rare outbursts of rhetoric" with long feathers that blocked the men's view. The article notes their increasing discomfort and reports that the following occurred as the performance began: "All hope for an afternoon's pleasure had about failed the two men, when the fair creatures, with one impulse, raised their hands to their heads, and, with a pressure on some magic spot, as it were, released the plumes from their bonnets, together with some side attachments of ribbon and other gear, and then, with a gentle tug, transformed the plumes into fans, with handles of the regulation length."[30] While the fan hat does not appear to have caught on, the account conveys a tongue-in-cheek attitude toward the problem of the theatre hat from the male spectators' perspective. Its appearance in the pages of the *Times* presupposes a familiarity with the problem on the part of the reader.

Women's theatre hats prompted adjustments in some of the city's theatrical institutions. "Pleading with Ladies' Hats," a *New York Times* article from 1886, reports that Daniel Frohman, manager of the Lyceum Theatre, would provide a special hat and cloak room for women in an effort to persuade them to give up their hats for the duration of the performance. The article describes the experiment as one "which interests every theatrical manger in the city. 'We'd like to see the plan successfully carried out,' all of them say, 'but we don't think it can be done.'" The article reports that representatives from Daly's Theatre, Madison Square Theatre, and Wallack's were consulted. They cited women's reluctance to hide showy hats, fear of catching cold, and the inconvenience of waiting for a checked hat to be returned after the performance as reasons that Frohman's reform would not succeed. "Suppose you're going in with your wife and the usher stops you and says 'your lady must remove her hat,'" theatre manager John Schoeffel is quoted as saying. "The average man from New Brunswick, N.J. will simply remark, 'Well, I guess not,' and will start away. No manager is going to let $3 get away in that way and the lady wears her hat into the theatre. That's the way the thing will work."[31] Given the numbers of women in the audience and the importance of selling tickets, Schoeffel assumed efforts to curb the problem were doomed to failure.

A subsequent newspaper account describes crowds of hatless ladies emerging from the new cloakroom at the Lyceum in excited tones, but the reform apparently did not take hold across the city.[32] A full ten years later, in 1896, the *Times* reported that the Metropolitan Opera House would request that women seated in the orchestra refrain from wearing hats during its coming season. Richard Neville, representative of the Opera House, is quoted as saying, "The reasons for such a move are apparent. Outside of the enhancement of the comfort of the audience it would make a much handsomer show for the ladies to leave their hats off." Again, the article reports that theatre managers across the city were "unanimous in the opinion that such a reform as the Opera House management is trying to secure would be a great boon to New York theatregoers. In the theatres, more than in the Opera House, the big hats are a nuisance and positively an obstruction. The managers of the theatres are interested in this aspect of the case more than the artistic side though they would not regret to see the occupants of the orchestra appear in full dress."[33] Again, while the Metropolitan Opera House may have succeeded in eliminating the theatre hat from the orchestra, the reform did not extend to other theatres in the city.

For some, proposed reforms to theatres' policies concerning ladies' hats raised complicated questions concerning class. While women's hats were widely recognized as a public nuisance in the theatre, they were also essential elements of the kind of streetwear sanctioned by etiquette experts. Respectable women walking through the city or using streetcars were required by their class status to wear hats. In a letter to the editor of *Life*, drama critic Alan Dale reacted to Daniel Frohman's proposed reforms at the Lyceum in 1886. He observes: "By furnishing ladies with hat and cloak rooms, managers have taken the first steps toward that evening dress which is possible in London and quite the contrary in America. I don't believe that managers want female audiences without hats. I submit that women in dark, high dresses, unhatted and unbonneted when in public places look very much like the fair frequenters of the cook's ball, the housemaid's treat, and other striking examples of high life below stairs."[34] Dale suggests that if ladies' hats are simply removed from the auditorium, that a large portion of the audience will look shabby and not quite respectable.

Dale goes on to argue that the Lyceum's policy pushes female members of the audience toward wearing full evening dress, which would not include a hat, but would preclude them from traveling to the theatre in streetcars. A woman in full evening dress would have to travel in a carriage or cab, meaning that a number of audience members would no longer be able to afford an evening's entertainment: "The Lyceum Theatre must get the entire city repaved before carriages and cabs will be plentiful enough to permit of an ordinary theatre goer indulging in the luxury. Imagine the impecunious youth of today taking the portly chaperone and her charge from Harlem to the theatre in a carriage! Think of his utter helplessness in the hands of the rabid cabmen!" Dale concludes by asserting: "This is a democratic city and a democratic country, and the lower classes . . . like to believe that they are not debarred from the luxuries of the upper strata." Although Dale acknowledges that some of the city's theatres ("Daly's, the Madison Square, and Wallack's") are primarily upper-class establishments, he asserts that there are at least twenty others where audiences are "mixed."[35] For Dale, tolerance of the ladies' theatre hat represented, at some level, a tolerance of class difference within the theatres of the city and he feared that their removal would signify the consolidation of the economically elite.

Numerous accounts of the theatre hat in the popular press provide examples of women striking back at men's discourteousness and lack of reciprocal concern, thus casting the debate in terms of gender conflict. In a 1901 article first published in the *New York Herald*, for instance, "the wife of a well known theatre manager" described an incident in which she planned to remove her hat before the performance began but was dissuaded from doing so when a man demanded it: "I determined then that I would most certainly not remove my hat. . . . After the curtain went up, the man called an usher who asked me to take off my hat. I told him that I had intended doing so but that the rude manner in which the man had spoken to me had caused me to change my mind. 'My hat stays on,' I said." She concludes her account by noting, "Most women of breeding will remove their hats when the curtain goes up, but they do not care to do so earlier, because they must hold the hat in their lap, and it is liable to be disarranged by other persons passing through the row before the performance is on. Am I right?"[36]

The presumptuousness of the man discussed in this article offended the woman who related the incident. He assumed that she would fail to remove her hat, and, by challenging her consideration, ensured that she did not.

Other discussions of the theatre hat by women describe different frustrations. "I do feel sorry for the woman who has to hold her best hat in her lap while independent men crowd past her," wrote "Bab," a New York correspondent for national newspapers, in 1897. "I do feel sorry for the woman who takes off her hat, knowing that her hair is not too well arranged, and that where she had expected to look smart she absolutely looks dowdy." This author makes a distinction between dressing for the theatre at night and during the day, but observes that women's hats are difficult to manage: "My method when I go to the theatre at night is to wear a black lace scarf over my head, which can be taken off. . . . Then at the matinee, I wear a hat or a bonnet that gets in nobody's way and I wouldn't take it off for the President of the United States for the simple reason that I could not get it on again."[37] While men's hats were short enough to be held comfortably in their laps, women's were large and, once removed, could become damaged by people passing back and forth through the aisles. Women also complained of lack of room in dressing spaces; and expressed impatience with the assumption that a large hat was indicative of vanity and a blind adherence to fashion. These women seem to have recognized that while the theatre hat was a legitimate problem for other spectators, they themselves were caught between conflicting demands and social expectations—looking appropriately fashionable, participating in cultural events, and being perfectly considerate of others.

Middle-class women in Gilded Age America found themselves in the midst of a rapidly transforming society as nineteenth-century respectability was warped and reshaped by early consumer capitalism. "As money translated into possession," Elaine Abelson observes, "a new sense of class identity was forged, not in production, but in consumption."[38] In the late nineteenth century, the theatre hat sat at the intersection of an older middle-class behavioral ethos and a newer middle-class consumer culture. The theatre hat functioned like a costume piece in that it embellished a gendered and classed performance of self. It enabled its wearer to be recognized as an up-to-date consumer. At the same time, it invited criticism for her failure, real or assumed, to adhere faithfully to social rules based on consideration of others. Public accounts of the hat in the popular press of the day are not limited to the hat alone, but are tangled up with debates about gender relations, class issues, institutional practices of theatres, and other cultural currents. Exploration of these discussions offers tantalizing glimpses of lived experience that surface within multiple discursive frames. In this way, the theatre hat enables us to consider ephemeral social practices within a fluid and shifting historical moment.

Notes

1. *The Chautauquan: A Weekly Newspaper*, March 1895.
2. "Those Big Hats Again," *New York Times*, March 28, 1897.
3. William Leach, "Transformations in a Culture of Consumption: Women and Department Stores, 1890–1925," *Journal of American History* 71, no. 2 (September 1984): 319.
4. Richard Butsch, "Bowery B'hoys and Matinee Ladies: The Re-Gendering of Nineteenth-Century American Theater Audiences," *American Quarterly* 46, no. 3 (September 1994): 374–75.
5. Joel Shrock, *The Gilded Age* (Westport, CT: Greenwood Press, 2004), xiii.
6. See Karen Halttunen, *Confidence Men and Painted Women: A Study of Middle-Class Culture in America, 1830–1870* (New Haven, CT: Yale University Press, 1982), and John Kasson, *Rudeness and Civility: Manners in 19th Century Urban America* (New York: Hill and Wang, 1990).
7. John H. Young, A. M., *Our Deportment or the Manners, Conduct, and Dress of the Most Refined Society* (Springfield, MA: W. C. King & Co., 1882), 15.
8. Abby Buchanan Longstreet, *Social Etiquette of New York* (New York: D. Appleton and Company, 1892), 8.
9. Young, *Our Deportment*, 14.
10. Mrs. H. O. Ward, *Sensible Etiquette of the Best Society: Customs, Manners, Morals, and Home Culture* (Philadelphia: Porter & Coates, 1878), xv.
11. Young, *Our Deportment*, 14.
12. "Woman's Theatre Manners," *New York Times*, February 23, 1896.
13. Leach, "Transformations," 325–26, 320.
14. Kathy Peiss, "Going Public: Women in Nineteenth-Century Cultural History," *American Literary History* 3, no. 4 (Winter 1991): 825.
15. Ibid. 824.
16. Elaine S. Abelson, *When Ladies Go A-Thieving: Middle-Class Shoplifters in the Victorian Department Store* (New York: Oxford University Press, 1989), 6, 11.
17. "Department Store Education," *New York Times*, December 20, 1903.
18. Kathy Peiss, "On Beauty . . . and the History of Business," *Enterprise & Society* 1, no. 3 (September 2000): 491.
19. Marla Schweitzer, *When Broadway Was the Runway: Theater, Fashion, and American Culture* (Philadelphia: University of Pennsylvania Press, 2009), 53.
20. Ibid., 51.
21. Stella Blum, ed., *Victorian Fashions and Costumes From Harper's Bazaar, 1867–1898* (New York: Dover Publications, 1974), 3, 77.
22. Shrock, *The Gilded Age*, 86.

23. "Her Point of View," *New York Times*, February 23, 1896.

24. "Urgent Plea For Birds," *New York Times*, December 3, 1897: 12.

25. Henry Ward Beecher, "Mr. Beecher's Letter, XI," *Christian Union* 35, no. 5 (February 3, 1887): 7.

26. William Dean Howells, "The Modern Crusade against the Theatre Hat," *Harper's Weekly* 19, no. 3 (March 1896): 230.

27. Mallon, "Dressing for the Theatre," *Ladies' Home Journal* 10, no. 2 (January 1893): 17.

28. S. L. Lewis, *Decorum: A Practical Treatise on Etiquette and Dress of the Best American Society* (New York: Union Publishing House, 1888), 280.

29. Mallon, "Dressing for the Theatre," 17.

30. "The New Theatre Hat," *New York Times*, November 13, 1898.

31. "Pleading with Ladies Hats," *New York Times*, December 7, 1886.

32. "Taking Off Their Hats," *New York Times*, January 5, 1887.

33. "Want Theatre Hats Removed," *New York Times*, November 15, 1896.

34. Alan Dale, "Drama," *Life* 8, no. 208 (December 23, 1886): 402.

35. Ibid., 402.

36. "When to Take Off Hats," *Washington Post*, May 26, 1901.

37. "Bab," "Theatre Hats: Bab Tells What Kind of Head Ornaments to Wear," *Los Angeles Times*, February 22, 1897.

38. Abelson, *When Ladies Go A-Thieving*, 34.

The RuPaul Effect

The Exploration of the Costuming Rituals of Drag Culture in Social Media and the Theatrical Performativity of the Male Body in the Ambit of the Everyday

Jorge Sandoval

THE COMMODIFICATION of drag by TV and social media—in other words, the commodified, queered, costumed male body presented through TV shows like *RuPaul's Drag Race* and all the social media coverage promoted by RuPaul's alumni and fan base on several online platforms—raises the concern of drag transforming from a traditional strategy for resistance into a trivialized and depoliticized representation of gender. Roger Baker, in his definition of drag, establishes "dissent" as a core characteristic of drag. He writes: "Drag is about many things. It is about clothes and sex. It subverts the dress codes that tell us what men and women should look like in our organized society. It creates tension and releases tension, confronts and appeases. It is about role playing and questions the meaning of both gender and sexual identity. It is about anarchy and defiance."[1] Drag has been culturally attached to gestures of resistance when referring to gender politics, as in the case of the Stonewall Riots in 1969,[2] and/or traditionally connected to theatrical forms such as drag queen performance or camp expressions in spaces considered theatrical. Theatrical drag, then, has historically served as a platform for the presentation of gender when other possibilities for expression were not socially acceptable. In her book *Vested Interests*, Marjorie Garber describes this situation: "The phenomenon of cross-dressing within theatrical representation, whether in the Dame and Principal Boy of the English pantomime, or in the popularity of films like *Victor Victoria*, *Tootsie* and *Some Like It Hot* . . . or indeed in the mode—increasingly chic today—of female impersonation as theatre, may be not only a commentary on the anxiety of gender roles in modern culture, but also—and perhaps primarily—a back-formation: a return to the problem of representation that underlies theatre itself."[3] Therefore, when considering the historically stigmatic position of homosexuality, professional drag done in nightclubs, gay bars, or street performances can also be considered a strategy for dissent. This was a strategy to normalize what otherwise would be considered deviant behavior. Esther Newton, in her book *Mother Camp*, talks about the professionalization of this subculture and the position that drag had in society: "Thus, insofar as female impersonators are professional drag queens, they are evaluated positively by gay people to the extent that they have perfected a subcultural skill and to the extent that gay people are willing to oppose the heterosexual culture. . . . On the other hand, they are despised because they symbolize and embody the stigma."[4] Drag has been part of our lives in a variety of forms from the ancient times of Greek theatre to the mundane medieval carnivalesque traditions seen and still carried into the present day when men dress as women with exaggerated female features. Not limited to theatre but heavily ingrained as part of the weaving of social interactions, men creating the illusion of femininity through drag has been part of our lives.[5] These expressions range from female impersonators, as in Chinese and Japanese theatre, looking for an ideal of femininity that aimed for no ambiguity, to modern Westernized performances of gender where female impersonators mostly looked for a larger-than-life, idealized illusion of femininity. It is also important to mention that, in this variety of forms, the use of the female impersonator as a comic figure, as in the nineteenth century when men dressed as women onstage, overtly showed that the artifice of the action was no longer a carnivalesque element of street celebrations but an important theatrical device.

From the theatrical drag queen entertaining in night clubs or at events, to the campy expressions of gay social and cultural life, all expressions seem to converge in the fact of drag being an integral part of societal activity.[6] Baker describes such activity: "[The drag queen] emerges from the mists of time and threads her way through the histories of all cultures and nations. She is present at solemn religious rites and kicks up her skirts at anarchic celebrations which mock authority and challenge the status quo. . . . The drag queen's unruly spirit still hovers unexpectedly over popular festivities, the fairs and celebration days held in villages and small towns with overstuffed bras and suspender belts."[7]

Whether we use it as a strategy of resistance or as a performance of identity, even camp at its most outrageous level is a social performance. Susan Sontag sums up the essence of camp as the "love of the unnatural: of artifice and exaggeration. And Camp is esoteric—something of a private code, a badge of identity even, among small urban cliques."[8] Baker describes female impersonation perceived as a camp expression but not separated from the idea of drag as performance: "So, from the beginning the idea of a man dressed as a woman was connected with social embarrassment; it would be some time before I realized that the popular assumption was that female impersonation equals homosexuality. But even some time later, when I finally identified myself as queer (the term used until late 1960s) and was becoming socialized into the gay circles of Nottingham in London, seeing anyone in drag—either on the stage or at private parties—was comparatively rare. When it did appear it was parodic, self-mocking—absolutely nothing to do with real women—and I began to understand it as part of that vocabulary which criticizes the mundane and everyday by transforming them into a glamorous, satirical frivolity; a process generally identified by the term 'camp.'"[9]

In today's world, the omnipresence of television and social media in the West has aided the widespread dissemination of such highly theatrical gestures. The conduits for such performances are television shows such as *RuPaul's Drag Race*, along with all the online postings from the show's alumni and its following. The spread of images and videos from the show and its performers has created the illusion of ordinariness, an illusory normality symptomatic of the need for online users to theatricalize the ambit of the everyday, and to drag their bodies when posting selfies online, thus transforming their bodies into a costume. I call this occurrence the RuPaul effect.

For the LGBTQ community, appearance has been a strong and effective strategy for dissent in homohysteria-driven societies; Eric Anderson defines homohysteria as "the fear of being homosexualized."[10] Traditionally, the LGBTQ community has been situated in Western societies within the frame of a hegemonic gender binary that portrays it as an entity outside the norm or integrated as a figure only seen through the lens of entertainment. Richard Dyer, in *The Culture of Queers*, comments on the controlled and commercially oriented image of this community in Western society: "We are presented there [on TV] as objects to be consumed. . . . We will know that we are gaining ground when serious presentation of our oppression on TV is such a commonplace that it coheres with the rest of the characterizations and presentations. At such time productions will only make sense if the forces we fight against are also presented seriously and accurately. However, commercially motivated arts do not present and endorse material that is critical of their own practice, including their contributions to gay oppression."[11]

Even though *RuPaul's Drag Race* is the creative product of a drag queen (RuPaul) who has placed theatrical drag on mainstream TV, I argue that the aim of the show is product-placement-driven, which dilutes drag expressions for social resistance into a theatricalized gesture of the everyday. Journalist Sharmin Kent describes RuPaul's main goal for the creation of the show: "But for RuPaul, drag was never the center of his life or even his career; instead it was simply a means to an end, a getaway to his destiny. 'I knew I had a personality, had something that I thought had value. . . . I just didn't know specifically what language or what venue it would be.'"[12] From the time of its first appearance in 2009 to now, this reality TV show has gained popularity in the LGBTQ community and other interested audiences able to access the show through specialty channels such as the OUT-TV network in Canada and the Logo TV network in the United States.[13] This viewership is certainly growing due to the show's structure and its characterization of the participants. The competition is based on the structures of other reality shows, like *Big Brother*, *America's Next Top Model*, and *Project Runway*, in which contestants are confined in a studio and taped while living nonscripted situations. Jim Daems, in *The Makeup of RuPaul's Drag Race*, quotes RuPaul's description of his show as a combination of several successful reality shows: "Tell Tyra [Banks] that the Queen has returned, and while you're at it have Heidi [Klum] clear the runway. I'm going to pump some 'realness' into reality. To be a winner on the show the contestants need to be a fashion designer, an American Idol, and a top model all rolled up into one. And definitely have to be smarter than a fifth grader."[14] This reality-type show is presented as entertainment, but it also claims to help the LGBTQ community to be more visible, and to promote tolerance among viewers outside this community;[15] however, the show presents a distorted view of a community where it appears that everybody does staged drag.

This inaccurate view of a community is presented in an environment where the main goal seems to be to sell an image as a product, along with more conventional products such as videos, books, and songs; a TV program with strong and obvious commercial elements such as product placement. A recurrent competitive challenge in the show, for instance, involves the making of a music video, as in the case of the final challenge on most seasons, in which contestants act in RuPaul's newest music video, in which RuPaul himself acts and sings as the lead. Other such challenges involve the contestants creating an advertising campaign (e.g., *RuPaul All Stars*, 2016), by which they promote RuPaul's videos or books. Such product placement is mostly communicated in a comedic manner in the form of a skit with parodic undertones that reinforces traditional views of drag.

From the performances of the "Mollies" in England in the 1700s[16] to the 1990s' music video "I Want to Break Free" by the British group

Queen, drag has been traditionally presented and perceived as staged comedy and outside the normative gender binary. In both cases, the impersonations focus on costumes and comedic actions, emanating from everyday life, that present the drag persona as a jester—like character in society: the Mollies wore nightgowns and nightcaps to dramatize the idea of women bearing children. Queen's attire reflects middle-class domestic life and activities. Each group concentrates on the parodic idea of such chores.

In the twenty-first century, *RuPaul's Drag Race* presents the LGBTQ community as out and proud, but, in fact, it places this community back into the traditional role of a gender outside society's dominant gender-binary format, as comic relief in and/or out of the view of the camera. A particular example from the show is the case of the Season 8 grand finale that presents all the contestants of that season onstage in a clearly staged/choreographed manner. When RuPaul notices the absence of a contestant, he quickly makes a cellphone call and arranges a last-minute replacement. The audience obviously expects it to be another contestant, possibly from a past season. Instead, he brings onstage a traditionally costumed male clown with all the stereotypical traits of what we imagine a clown would look like: big shoes, white clown makeup, red nose, and a curly, colorful wig. The clown places himself within the space of the drag queens as one of them. Bianca Del Rio, a past winner from the show who stands next to the clown, acknowledges the clown's presence and comments: "I like your makeup," alluding to the exaggerated makeup traditionally worn by drag queens. As this is, of course, a calculated and staged joke, it certainly becomes emblematic of the place in which this community has been repositioned in the world of entertainment and, subliminally, in the minds of the viewers, where drag exists as a theatrical form, only understood as a camp expression connected to homosexuality and gender misfit. Roger Baker, in *Drag*, summarizes the traditional perception of drag from the time that such activity has been recorded: "The female impersonator had become a comic figure, a creature of burlesque and parody at the end of the seventeenth century. . . . If the nineteenth century created a female impersonator who was an almost cartoon-like figure of low comedy, the twentieth century's contribution has been to add glamour and today's dame is likely to shimmer and glitter just as much as her sisters the drag queens but always with the essential added edge of caricature."[17]

From the perspective of Baker's thoughts, *RuPaul's Drag Race* presents a variety of drag styles that range from female impersonators like Derrick Barry in Season 8 (a Britney Spears impersonator) to the conceptual drag of Sasha Velour in Season 9 (Sasha Steinberg).[18] Such diversity is somehow standardized in the show through the element of comedy. Dramatic situations occurring during challenges or in the section "Untucked," for instance, are edited so contestants are presented as competitive or stressed, and most times these exchanges are treated in a comedic way. *RuPaul's Drag Race All Stars* Season 2, Episode 2 presents a situation in which contestant Phi Phi O'Hara faces elimination and is presented as desperate and gossipy. Her fate in the competition is in the hands of contestant Alaska, who seems to have an alliance with two other contestants, Roxxy and Detox (together known as "Rolaskatox").[19] Such exchanges are carefully edited to give audiences comedic instances even when the contestants are presented backstage and not in their drag personae.

RuPaul's Drag Race's main conceptual goal is to find "America's Next Drag Superstar." Based on this premise, the show is already following dominant views of gender, such as the search for idealized beauty through other reality shows, such as *America's Next Top Model*, and beauty pageants, like *Miss Universe* among many others, in which the combination of talent and beauty creates the perfect archetype of femininity in a binary-gendered society.

Following this pattern, the show presents the contestants (gay men) at activities mainly connected to the dominant views of masculinity and femininity in homohysteria-driven societies. The show makes it evident that such talents are seen as the core of drag's identity as promoted for men and women in gender binary-oriented societies. These talents prove the queens' ability to excel in certain tasks that are presented as the traits of "America's Next Drag Superstar," tasks like sewing costumes and making wigs, modeling, and, of course, creating a hyperbolic image of femininity. The issue here is the fact that viewers and fans receive a limited and guided view of gender, where feminine and masculine are dominant, leaving alternative gender expressions out of scope.

Consequently, to make sure the viewer understands the fact that the contestants are men impersonating women by cross-dressing as part of the show, the program presents the show's host and the contestants in male clothing first and foremost, and as the show unfolds they transform into their drag personae, which emblematically highlights the idea that gender is a defined social construct. RuPaul, the host, reinforces this narrative as he challenges the contestants at the beginning of every show with his catchy phrase, "Gentlemen, start your engines and may the best woman win." By presenting this perspective on gender, the show establishes a single, binary view of gender that does not leave space for alternative gender expressions. Due to this premise, trans contestants, such as Peppermint in Season 9, most often present themselves as men dressing in women's clothes.

The Queered Costumed Male Body

I wish to explore briefly the connection between appearance and the theatricality of the body by examining the term "Muscle Mary." This term, used in gay culture worldwide, defines a man who looks, according to the dominant views of gender, like a "masculine" man with a defined and muscular body, but it is still connected with homosexual behavior.

Being defined as a "Muscle Mary" implies a parody, a representation of a normative masculinity accepted and not contested. Socially, being a "Muscle Mary" grants one some masculine capital and allows one to navigate parallel to the heterosexual ambit and, for the most part, "allows" one to inhabit the normative world of men.[20] An example of this dynamic is Russian Facebook personality Pavel Petel, with his hyper-masculinity understood as drag.[21] His drag persona is so unapologetic that it passes as normal in the space of normative sexual behavior. His body, big, muscular, and tanned, with masculine features, creates a performative gesture that brings him into the world of the everyday as the real thing, a theatricalized version of masculinity, a denaturalized self. In the case of *RuPaul's Drag Race*, there is a group that represents this kind of masculinity: the Pit Crew, also known as The Scruff. This group of muscular men appear on every episode, dressed only in their underwear, assisting RuPaul and the contestants. They have no dialogue and their function is to appear as what rupaulsdragrace.wikia.com defines as "eye candy."[22] Such characters use their masculine capital and function metaphorically as the anchor that balances the gender binary in the show and for the viewers. These Muscle Mary–like characters present themselves as objects of desire for both men and women viewers, and their bodies serve as costumes for the performance of gender.

RuPaul's Drag Race, like Pavel Petel, disseminates a theatricalized version of a culture that existed out and before the show. This dissemination reinforces rather than expands upon traditional views on gender. *RuPaul's Drag Race* promotes the re-creation of extreme views of femininity by online followers of the show (as in the case of fan Empressthetemptress) in a casual, theatrical manner that unintentionally emphasizes hegemonic views of gender reinforced by dress. Judith Butler, in her book *Bodies That Matter*, explains how hegemonic privilege functions: "Heterosexual privilege operates in many ways, and two ways in which it operates include naturalizing itself and rendering itself as the original and the norm."[23] Butler's statement allows me to think of these two different groups and gestures as one; both "Muscle Mary" types and RuPaul's fans use their bodies as a theatrical space to perform without being subversive. From this perspective, male bodies present two types of performance: the performance of gender in Butlerian terms and the performance of gender in a theatrical fashion, both presented simultaneously and difficult to separate.

To define the performance of drag, I would say that this expression is a mundane way to appropriate and theatricalize the characteristics of a specific gender that is different from our own. Drag, then, allows us to appropriate, wear, and gender an impersonation. From this perspective, drag becomes a performance of gender rather than an imitation of an original gender, whatever that would be. Therefore, I see *RuPaul's Drag Race* followers' drag expressions as having no clear position as to which is the dominant or the imitation of the norm, but rather as a theatrical gesture of gender being performed without any assumptions about which one is the original.

Cyber Drag

RuPaul's Drag Race has a big presence in social media and a big following through the show's website and Facebook page.[24] The use of social media by fans of shows like *RuPaul's Drag Race* influences the way that fans of the show interact with each other and present their bodies online.

With the creation and vast use of this new space called "cyberspace," the term "embodiment" certainly takes on a new role and a first-row placement in our society. For the purpose of this essay, embodiment is understood as the body being a manifestation of cultural entities.[25] The wide use of cyberspace for the negotiation of everyday life has made the term embodiment even more relevant. Social media and interactive technologies have made it possible for us to embody this negotiation in a variety of forms. John R. Suler, in his book *Psychology of the Digital Age*, mentions such embodiment: "Of all the many ways people might express themselves in cyberspace, the most embodied experience is the avatar. It is a unique fusion of the identity and sensory dimensions of cyberpsychology architecture."[26] As regular social media users, as soon as we get the advantage of access to cyberspace, we create metaphorical avatars[27] and set ourselves to the task of inhabiting this new space to present, represent, and misrepresent ourselves. From the moment we were able to occupy this new space, we took it and populated it.[28]

We have inhabited this space looking for information and searching for other users with similar interests. We quickly discovered the possibility of seeing what other people do and think, but, most importantly, we discovered the act of being seen ourselves.[29] The realization here is that we can inhabit this virtual world and embody it. This creates a new type of space for the performance of the body, a space that has turned every spectator into a performer and a peeper whose desire to watch is as big and fulfilling as the act of performing her/his identity for an audience. Hal Niedzviecki summarizes this phenomenon: "When we peep on each other, we experience the thrill of performance."[30] Social media has added to our everyday life this urge to know what others are doing and at the same time, we can't wait to tell the world what we are doing.

We, the users, have created the need to live and to function in parallel worlds, oscillating between real time and space, and cyberspace. Technological developments have allowed us to be in cyberspace as if we are moving and acting in real time; however, this illusion creates conflicts when it comes to representation. It is suddenly very easy to reinvent ourselves and to create a new and fresh identity. This reinvention can be relatively innocuous, as in the case of presenting our happy and positive selves every time we post some image or comment on Facebook or Twitter, or as dark as misrepresenting ourselves online for evil purposes such as cyber bullying, where the virtual body is used as a shield with the sole purpose being to harm.

The Male Costumed Body and Its Inherent Theatricality

To discuss the inherent theatricality of the costumed body in a non-theatrical setting, it is important to define what dress means in the ambit of the everyday and to examine the position of the male body vis-à-vis the concepts of dress and costume. Joanne Entwistle states that clothing is essential to being a person. This refers to the differentiation between animal and human. Entwistle describes our relationship with clothing as the one that defines our conceptions of personhood, urbanity, and bodily integrity. She describes our relationship with dress: "Conventions of dress transform flesh into something recognizable and meaningful to a culture and are also the means by which bodies are made 'decent,' appropriate and acceptable within specific contexts."[31]

In simple terms, she might say "clothes make the man"; however, this sartorial, production-based conception of the body in society reduces the body to an equation of power and social constructs that is subordinated to the system of consumerism. Exploring the body in a wider range allows me to look at the reiterative and reflective quality of the body in action when it exchanges gestures with other bodies and its environment. These gestures, one of them being the gaze, become the articulation of an inherent theatricality that rearticulates its nature every time it moves; it exchanges with other bodies and situations. This aleatoric exchange alters immensely the relationship of the body and its surroundings. For instance, posting a headless picture of oneself can activate the gaze and turn this gesture into an exchange between the gaze and the gazer. It is in this very instance that we can have an expectation of a performance.

Aoife Monks, in *Costume*, talks specifically about the tight connection between artificially constructed identities onstage and the ones created outside the stage. She writes: "However, even as [Judith] Butler distinguishes between artificially produced identity onstage and invisibly produced identity on the street, the role that theatre costume plays in producing these ideal standards of bodily conduct remains important. . . . Costume can therefore be understood as a mechanism of the Real, a place in which legitimate and illegitimate bodies are invented, formed and produced."[32] To go deeper into the theatricality of the male costumed body, it is important to visit the idea of dress in society and how this performative gesture impacts social relations and underlines theatricality in the ambit of the mundane, when the elements of design and performance are added into the equation.

Dress, as we know it, has primarily separated us from animals. We have used clothing to protect our bodies from the elements, but this primary need was also rapidly supplemented by the use of garments for modesty, adornment, and the production of power relations in society. We quickly learned how to enhance our position as humans and to distance ourselves from the beast as we gave cultural connotations to what we wear and how we wear it. Dressing becomes, then, an identity signifier in which the body becomes a space where we perform what Amir Ben Porat calls "our affective, experiential and symbolic selves."[33]

According to Ben Porat's categorization, we perform our affective selves through cathartic experiences during which our bodies create mechanisms to bond with our cultural environment.[34] We, devoted social media users, cheer, scream, give thumbs up or down, give happy or upset emoticons to our friends, and move in a carnivalesque choreography that resembles a pagan ceremony. In addition to this catharsis that we wish to achieve, we, as humans, have an innate need to belong, and one way to bond is through clothing that connects us symbolically with our ideological environment. We follow fashion trends, bond with national colors that create citizenship, or, in the case of the fans of celebrities such as RuPaul, we emulate language patterns and fashion and create memes that generate unique signifiers with which only the same group can identify. This works together with our experiential selves by creating cognitive relations with the environment and our dressed bodies; we justify our placement in this environment; we belong there and the identification is justified by the created need. This experiential relation with the environment translates into a bonding experience where we establish our identity by creating links with identities equal or opposite to ours.

RuPaul's Drag Race fans' costumed bodies presented in social media (Facebook, Instagram, and Twitter, among several)[35] and inspired by looks and trends from RuPaul's contestants create a queer space that inserts in the ambit of the everyday a new point of reference from which to read the fans' bodies.

The moment when these queered bodies are juxtaposed with spaces such as cyberspace, the street, or the traditional heteronormative space of the heterosexual body, the costumed body becomes emblematic, denaturalizes itself, and exposes the innate theatricality of the body. Such embodiment transforms the action of costuming into a performative instance that unifies all levels of discourse and extends the innate theatricality of the queered body to the ambit of the everyday.

As this denaturalized view of drag disseminates, other gender expressions that are not meant to be theatrical are considered as such. Online fan pages such as Fanpop.com or imgrum.org, an online Instagram web viewer, among many, express their admiration for RuPaul's contestants' beauty and skillful glamorization of the body; however, this same skillful exaggeration of femininity becomes widely disseminated and creates a distorted view of the LGBTQ community and reinforces unrealistic views of femininity.

An example is the image of a fan (Empressthetemptress) on the *RuPaul's Drag Race* New Zealand fan page,[36] in which he costumes his body with a tight corset that presents an unrealistic body proportion. The fan photo mirrors the almost fantastical silhouette presented by Drag Queen Violet Chachki in *RuPaul's Drag Race* Season 7.[37]

The costumed male body in the context of reality TV and social media, then, becomes the stage for eroticism and sexual identification, where the idea of embodiment becomes part of the event. Therefore, I ask: is the mediatized costumed male body taking the role of the sexed object, offering, metaphorically, his flesh and sexual identity to the spectator? Are these theatricalized bodies creating gestures and relationships with their surroundings that shape their audiences' identities? In attempting to answer these questions, it is important to present concisely how the costumed body functions and objectifies itself in the world of social media.

In postmodern society, the act of performing the body in cyberspace has become both an everyday life event and a performative act. We watch reality TV and participate in highly charged voyeuristic activities such as posting and sharing photos, videos, messages, or comments in spaces like Facebook, Twitter, and Instagram, among others. Our society has become a consumer of voyeuristic instances where we perform and participate on a global stage. Hal Niedzviecki, in *The Peep Diaries*, summarizes this twenty-first-century cultural phenomenon: "Peep coalesces the sensibility of twenty-first-century techno society into a never-ending spectacle of bodies and sounds bared in the name of entertainment, self-betterment, and instantaneous recognition. Peep is a portal into a collective consciousness no longer content to sit on the sidelines and watch: We want to do."[38]

Peep culture has facilitated, and made more and more complex, the role of the body in cyberspace vis-à-vis traditional notions of theatrical performance. The idea of performing gender through imagery created for virtual space establishes a new paradigm created by virtual culture and performativity. Based on this premise, images of virtual headless bodies posted on sites like Facebook or Grindr have become the epitome of the postmodern theatrical performance. Drag expressions displayed in cyberspace, inspired by TV and social media and trickled down to everyday spheres, present a distorted view of gender based on a decontextualized body appearance. Once the concept of gender has been trivialized, as in the case of RuPaul's reality show, the inherent theatricality of the everyday is activated and objectifies the costumed body of social media fans.[39]

RuPaul's Drag Race's hyperbolic presentation of femininity through costuming (as in the case of contestant Violet Chachki, mentioned earlier on this paper), I propose, is decontextualized and disseminated by social media. Such hyperbolic imagery perpetuates the dominant gender binary in western societies and revives the narrative of bodies being commodified. This places the bodies of the drag queens in the show as entities for consumption, bodies that have lost their power of resistance. They no longer hold the power to create a narrative of dissent since they are promoting and perpetuating the same values they are traditionally fighting against. We see this when contestants, like Violet Chachki or Miss Fame (Season 7), present a hyperbolic view of femininity for their drag personae: unrealistic waist suppression created by corsets, overly slim silhouettes, burlesque-like makeup, and pasty-pale skin. Even though Violet Chachki is a character presented in the show, his own body also presents and promotes unrealistic proportions that distort views of what is masculine and feminine. Even the thought of the contestants' male queered costumed bodies being considered as new masculinities, coexisting along with heterosexual views of the body, is problematic here since the contestants' queered costumed bodies are replicating values already rooted and working for the dominant normative views of gender.

Hypothetically, the idea of the theatricality of the costumed gendered body and the transgression created by the queered male body in drag transform the gesture of costuming into a performative act where the costumed queered bodies, using Alan Read's terms, "exoticise the domestic rather than domesticate the exotic."[40] An example of this would be the section in every show when the contestants apply their makeup in front of the mirrors before the final challenge. While they prepare, they exchange personal thoughts and anecdotes of their personal lives. This action creates a juxtaposition of the fantastic with the real. When audiences watch this section, they receive the impression that the fantastic is the real. Therefore, when audiences reproduce such gestures in the realm of the everyday, they remain within this realm. They are usually not transposed or manipulated for consideration or used as a traditional theatrical expression. They remain an everyday gesture and are only understood within these specific parameters; however, they can inspire traditional theatrical forms. The fans and followers of RuPaul's show transform their bodies based on the show's manipulation of the body. The body, then, becomes an asexual identity only used as a costume to perpetuate gender through a magnified and stereotypical image of gender.

The RuPaul Effect

Cross-dressing has been part of many societies in the past, is part of our present, and will be part of our future. Transforming the body into a different representation of the self has been part of culture. Views on cross-dressing have mostly been perceived through the discourse of sexual binaries. Roger Baker, in *DRAG*, explains the effect that theatrical drag on TV in the 1980s and 1990s had on the audience: "When Lily Savage or Dame Edna Everage stalk onto the stage and fascinate their terrorized audience they are recreating for us one of the oldest of our totems, becoming emblems of the unseen but ever present tension between order and chaos."[41] Baker's statement, valid still in many societies ruled by binary views on gender, is less emblematic since social media has opened the door for average Johns and Janes to become "Dame Ednas." Even with the idea of gender fluidity, most narratives about cross-dressing orbit around the idea of dressing as the opposite sex.

Based on established Western binary views of gender in society, cross-dressing refers mostly to the meaning associated with the clothing and/or the transformation that our body goes through to establish an identity and a new sense of self. From Greek theatre to the digital era, cross-dressing has been attached to the transformation of the body into its opposite.

Traditionally, theatre has become a niche where the breaking of the rules is not only accepted but promoted; from carnivalesque medieval expressions to Shakespearean theatre to *RuPaul's Drag Race* in the twenty-first century, cross-dressing has been accepted and cultivated as a theatrical form. The advent of the Web 2.0 and interactive technologies has drastically changed this tradition. Social media has made it possible for anyone to present themselves in whatever form they please. Ironically, social media has allowed the everyday person to express herself/himself, but it has also created the need to perform, to see and be seen by our neighbors. Social media has allowed us to become a performer and producer anytime we "drag" our bodies when we make and send a selfie. We use our body as a costume to perform. *RuPaul's Drag Race* has facilitated the dissemination of gender expressions due to its popularity and worldwide exposure; however, these expressions, which I call the RuPaul effect, have remained linked to the theatrical expression of reality TV.

Conclusion

The space of the fans' costumed body, inspired by *RuPaul's Drag Race* and its contestants, is utilized as a scenographic space in which every fragment is used to create a theatricality that affects the viewer and the actant. The body is being disturbed by means of shaping, such as waist suppression as in the cases of Violet Chachki and fan Empressthetemptress, and created in a very dramaturgical manner.

The sartorial alteration of the body with fabrics, colors, and textures brings the body into a state where gender naturalization occurs as the body goes through a transforming process. Judith Butler explains such naturalization: "The origin requires its derivations in order to affirm itself as an origin, for origins only make sense to the extent that they are differentiated from that which they produce as derivatives. Hence, if it were not for the notion of the homosexual as copy, there would be no construct of heterosexuality as origin."[42]

Such exaggeration of the anatomy through the amplification of colors, shapes, and form through costume, hair, and makeup, and even the alteration of the male form through waist suppression or surgery (as in the cases of contestants like Sharon Needles, Season 1, or Chad Michaels, Season 4),[43] renders the body into an ideal space, a space where the imitation of itself becomes the original. The show and its contestants operate in such a way that the male queered costumed body naturalizes the self or, in other words, creates the illusion of normality by promoting established views of gender when instituting, as a rule, a view of the world based on a gender binary. The RuPaul effect, then, operates through the cancellation of the body's possibilities for resistance and embedding a theatricality that social media followers of the show take as the real.[44]

Notes

1. Roger Baker, *DRAG: A History of Female Impersonation in the Performing Arts* (London: Cassell, 1994), 18.

2. Baker describes how drag became a major political actant during the Stonewall riots: "But come the heady days of the late 1960s politics had also become fun, and being gay had become increasingly political—it was drag queens who were among the fiercest fighters during New York's Stonewall Riots in 1969." Ibid., 239.

3. Marjorie Garber, *Vested Interests: Cross Dressing and Cultural Anxiety* (New York: Routledge, 1997), 40.

4. Esther Newton, *Mother Camp: Female Impersonators in America* (Chicago: University of Chicago Press, 1979), 104. The author talks about "the stigma" as the idea of cross-dressing equaling homosexuality and homosexuality equaling deviant behavior.

5. Baker explains: "In the high drama of ancient Rome and Athens she [the drag queen] was there to facilitate the ceremonies of rebirth and fertility. In the low theatre of the common people she has leered and flaunted her sexual ambiguity. Among the Native American tribes of North America she has, as a berdache, being institutionalized as an awesome representation of a third sex, one gifted with magical powers and invested with divine authority, uniting male and female into the undifferentiated sexuality of the primal creative force." Baker, *DRAG*, 23.

6. Baker describes the presence of Drag expressions as part of the dynamics of the everyday: "To suggest that our awareness of drag in its various forms is higher now than it was a quarter of a century ago is an understatement. Sometimes it seems that every time we glance at a colour magazine, watch television, go to the cinema or submit to a pop video we are confronted by some aspect of cross-dressing." Ibid., 10.

7. Ibid., 23–24.

8. Susan Sontag, "Notes on 'Camp,'" in *Camp: Queer Aesthetics and the Performing Subject: A Reader*, ed. Fabio Cleto (Ann Arbor: University of Michigan Press, 2002), 53.

9. Baker, *DRAG*, 2.

10. Eric Anderson, "The Rise and Fall of Western Homohysteria," *Journal of Feminist Scholarship* 1 (Fall 2011): 87.

11. Richard Dyer, *The Culture of Queers* (New York: Routledge, 2002), 24.

12. Sharmin Kent, "How 'Drag Race' Gave RuPaul a Comeback—And Made Him a Next Generation Oprah," *Thinkprogress*, October 11, 2013 (accessed June 18, 2017), https://thinkprogress.org/how-drag-race-gave-rupaul-a-comback-andmade-him-a-next-generation-oprah-21ac812914d8.

13. Blogs like *TV By the Numbers* and *Deadline Hollywood* reported the highest viewership in the history of the show with nearly one million viewers on

the Season 9 opening show (2017). Denise Petski, "RuPaul's Drag Race Draws Nearly 1M Viewers in VH1 Debut," *Deadline Hollywood*, March 27, 2017, http://deadline.com/2017/03/rupauls-drag-race-ratings-records-1million-viewers-season-9-premiere-vh1-1202053113 (accessed June 18, 2017). Alex Welch, "Friday Cable Ratings: RuPaul's Drag Race' Ticks Back Up," *TV by the Numbers*, May 30, 2017, http://tvbythenumbers.zap2it.com/daily-ratings/friday-cable-ratings-may-26–2017 (accessed June 18, 2017).

14. Jim Daems, *The Makeup of RuPaul's Drag Race: Essays on the Queen of Reality Show* (Jefferson, NC: McFarland & Company, 2014), 6.

15. In an article following an interview with RuPaul, Sharmin Kent discusses RuPaul's comments about helping the LGBTQ community: "And with *RuPaul's Drag Race*, he has found his calling: extolling the virtues of personal empowerment. He spends most of each episode . . . doling out advice from beauty to relationships. Ending each episode of *Drag Race* with an Oprahfied affirmation: 'If you can't love yourself, how in hell you gonna love anybody else? Can I get an amen!'" Kent, "How 'Drag Race' Gave RuPaul a Comeback."

16. Roger Baker describes a group of men in the UK dressing as women who called themselves "Mollies." These accounts were published in the *London Spy* between 1698 and 1709. The report describes this group as so "totally destitute of all masculine attributes that they prefer to behave as women . . . [and] would be dressed in a woman's nightgown with a silken nightcap, and thus represent a woman bearing a child." Baker, *DRAG*, 99–100.

17. Ibid., 161–62.

18. Sasha Velour, in an interview with Kevin Ritchie for *NOW* magazine, defines his style of drag as "conceptual." He describes his drag as "a performance of gender that allows people to push outside the binary." He adds: "I'm certainly not inventing anything new with drag, but I represent a world of drag that maybe hasn't had its moment yet on the show." Kevin Ritchie, "RuPaul's Drag Race snatches the spotlight," *Now Magazine*, June 21, 2017, https://nowtoronto.com/movies/features/rupaul-s-drag-race-sasha-velour-shea-coulee (accessed June 18, 2017).

19. Nicole Silverberg, "RuPaul's Drag Race All Stars Recap: Snatch Your Tears," September 2, 2016, http://www.vulture.com/2016/09/drag-race-all-stars-recap-season2-episode-2.html (accessed June 20, 2017).

20. Eric Anderson defines masculine capital: "If a male acts in accord with the five tenets mentioned above [1] not associating with homosexuality. 2) not associating with femininity. 3) being a big wheel. 4) being a sturdy oak, and 5) giving them hell] he can be described as attempting to raise his masculine capital." Eric Anderson, *In The Game: Gay Athletes and the Cult of Masculinity* (Albany: State University of New York Press, 2005), 24.

21. Pavel Petel is a Russian Facebook and Instagram celebrity famous for his impressive physique and outrageous looks. He mainly uses elements of drag in his postings and performances. Instagram: pavel_petel1, Facebook page: Pavel Petel, Twitter feed: https:www.//twitter.com/PavelPetel.

22. RuPaul's Drag Race Wiki, Rupalsdragrace.wikia.com/wiki/Pit_Crew (accessed July 19, 2017).

23. Judith Butler, *Bodies That Matter* (New York: Routledge Classics, 2011), 85.

24. Official Facebook page, Twitter feed, and Instagram: https://www.facebook.com/rupaulsdragrace (1,967,832 likes as of July 19, 2017; 718,000 followers as of February 15, 2018); https://instagram.com/RuPaulsDRagRace (1.3 million followers as of July 19, 2017).

25. Joanne Entwistle describes embodiment as the body being a "medium of expression since it is heavily mediated by culture, and expresses the social pressure brought to bear on it. Indeed, the body becomes a symbol of its cultural location." Joanne Entwistle and Elisabeth Wilson, eds., *Body Dressing* (Oxford: Berg, 2001), 40.

26. John R. Suler, *Psychology of the Digital Age: Humans Become Electric* (Cambridge: Cambridge University Press, 2005), 226.

27. "Avatar" is a term first used by science fiction novelist Neal Stephenson in his novel *Snow Crash*. Suler defines it as "the perfect term to capture the unique online experience that began in the late 1980s, when inventors of digital media constructed graphical worlds in which people could create and maneuver visual representations of themselves as a way to interact with the environment and the people in it." Ibid., 226.

28. Suler explains this development: "In 1993, with the introduction of the popular graphical browser Mosaic, the web became visual. In addition to reading and writing, people could now see images, including graphics and photographs. Sound files and videos followed. Webpages grew more sophisticated in visual, conceptual, and functional design. Due to the enhanced sensory qualities of this fascinating web, more people began going online, forming many different kinds of relationships, groups, and communities, a movement that bloomed when the Internet became commercialized with the relaxing of government restrictions on its use." Ibid., 3.

29. Hal Niedzviecki describes this need: "Though there may be significant generational divides, we're all part of Peep culture. We're learning to love watching ourselves and our neighbors. . . . Anyone who's ever lost few hours clicking on the profile pictures of friends and friends' friends knows what Peep is all about. It's about wanting to know everything about everyone and, in turn, wanting to make sure that everyone knows everything about you." Hal Niedzviecki, *The Peep Diaries: How We're Learning to Love Watching Ourselves and Our Neighbors* (San Francisco: City Lights Books, 2009), 4, 8.

30. Ibid., 4.

31. Entwistle and Wilson, *Body Dressing*, 33.

32. Ali Maclaurin and Aoife Monks, eds., *Costume: Readings in Theatre Practice* (New York: Palgrave Macmillan Education, 2015), 108.

33. Amir Ben Porat, "Football Fandom: A Bounded Identification," *Soccer and Society* 11, no. 3 (May): 277–90.

34. When discussing Michel Foucault's concept of the socially processed body, Entwistle also mentions these levels of experience that connect to Amir Ben Porat's levels of identification. She writes about Foucault's account of the socially processed body and provides analysis of the way in which the body is talked about

and acted on but does not provide an account of dress as it is lived, experienced, and embodied by individuals. Entwistle and Wilson, *Body Dressing*, 40.

35. See note 24 for the show's official social media URLs. In addition: Imgrum.org, www.dragofficial.com, and Fanpop.com (accessed July 19, 2017).

36. Empressthetemptress Instagram, https://www.instagram.com/empress.the.temptress/?hl=en (accessed August 14, 2017).

37. See violetchachki on Instagram and/or violetchachki.net.

38. Niedzviecki, *The Peep Diaries*, 18.

39. Alan Read explains the inherent theatricality of the ambit of the everyday: "Theatre's relation with everyday life remains a domain of unwritten negotiation, a domain where the licences granted to theatre are implicit rather than explicit and in their apparent absences are all the stronger in their influence over what theatre can do." Alan Read, *Theatre and the Everyday: An Ethics of Performance* (New York: Routledge, 1995), 9.

40. Ibid., 7.

41. Baker, *DRAG*, 23.

42. Judith Butler, "Imitation and Gender Insubordination," in *The Lesbian and Gay Studies Reader*, ed. Henry Abelove, Michèle Aina Barale, and David M. Halperin (New York: Routledge, 1993), 313.

43. "Keeping track of the contestants plastic surgeries," *RuPaul's Drag Race Reddit*, https://www.redit.com/r/rupaulsdragrace/comments/1tizic/keeping_track_of_the_contestants__plastic_surgeries (accessed July 20, 2017).

44. Tim Winfred, "RuPaul's Drag Race Has Sort of Killed Drag for Queens Who Are Not on the Show," *Queerty*, April 25, 2016, https://www.queerty.com/rupauls-drag-race-has-sort-of killed-drag-forqueens-who-are-not-on-the-show-20160425 (accessed June 20, 2017).

A Brand New Day on Broadway

The Genius of Geoffrey Holder's Artistry and His Intentional Evocation of the African Diaspora

Gregory S. Carr

IN 1975, BROADWAY was hit by a storm that was bigger than the one that swept Dorothy Gale away from Kansas and into the Land of Oz. That storm was a musical called *The Wiz*, directed by the inimitable Geoffrey Holder (1930–2014), whose illustrious career spanned four decades as an actor, director, painter, and costume designer. After *The Wiz* suffered a series of disastrous previews at the Mechanic Theatre in Baltimore and the Fisher Theatre in Detroit, Holder took over the reins of the latter production from director Gilbert Moses. What happened afterward was nothing short of a miracle. Rallying around Holder, choreographer George Faison, composer/lyricist Charlie Smalls, and librettist William F. Brown joined forces to heal a fractured cast after Gilbert's departure. After affectionate hugs and chanting positive mantras failed to win over the cast, Holder decided to use his own money to purchase food and drink to bring the cast closer together.[1] The plan worked to get the production to New York, but it could not prevent an inauspicious Broadway opening, with *The Wiz* widely panned by critics. The production nearly closed amid deepening financial woes. However, the ultimate success of the musical did not come via flashy marketing but from old-fashioned word-of-mouth promotion.[2] Sandra Manley, a press agent for the show, gave away limitless press tickets to radio personalities, newspaper writers, and television agents in exchange for their promotion of the struggling show.[3]

While the debuts of fifteen-year-old Stephanie Mills as Dorothy and eighteen-year-old Hinton Battle as the Scarecrow were heralded as breakout performances, Holder's innovative and inspired direction quickened the pace of the show. Not only did *The Wiz* become a runaway hit, but it received a number of awards along the way. The show ran from January 1975 to May 1977 at the Majestic Theatre, and then from May 1977 to January 1979 at the Broadway Theatre, for a total of 1,672 performances.[4] The show garnered Holder two Tony Awards, for Best Direction of a Musical and for Best Costume Designs.[5] Although the iconic costumes from the film *The Wizard of Oz* (1939) have become touchstones of American cultural memory, Holder created new costumes for *The Wiz* with great flamboyance and aplomb, giving the story a new cultural context. Evocation of the African Diaspora played a huge role in making Holder's costume designs for *The Wiz* a success.

People of African descent have been speaking in code, writing with hidden messaging, and dealing in double entendres since they before they began arriving in the New World as a result of the transatlantic slave trade. Enslaved Africans commonly used "call and response" songs on the slave ships to communicate with one another. A seemingly innocuous Negro spiritual such as "Steal Away," which appeared to be a melodious plantation ditty and a possible pious call for prayer, turned out to be a coded invitation to join Harriet Tubman's Underground Railroad, a musical bolt toward freedom. In this tradition of the African Diaspora, librettist William F. Brown, composer/lyricist Charlie Smalls, and producer Ken Harper took an American classic like *The Wizard of Oz*, famous as both a book and a movie, and updated it for a 1970s African American audience. And in a continuation of the Diaspora motif, Holder planted relevant evocations of the black aesthetic in his costume designs and in his use of Afro-Caribbean musical instruments, African American historical and artistic references, and Afrofuturistic allusions and motifs.

The celebration of Afro-Caribbean musical instruments and clothing designs are evident in Holder's costumes for *The Wiz*. Holder fashioned the Tin Man's oilcan from a *güiro*, in homage to a popular West Indian musical instrument. Janell Hobson of Albany State University calls attention to the importance of the *güira*, denoting its unique ties to the island of Hispaniola, the locale of the Dominican Republic and Haiti.[6] While the güiro is "a serrated gourd or calabash," the *güira* is a "metal scraper used for Dominican merengue, scraped with a metal fork that resembles an Afro pick."[7] The güiro is a percussive instrument that is often played by scraping the güira across the surface of the güiro for a "grated" sound. The güira is often incorporated into many Latin and non-Latin percussion ensembles.[8]

Merengue, the national dance of the Dominican Republic and closely related to its island neighbor Haiti's Mereng, descended from the musical roots of the Bantus of Madagascar. Merengue is thought to have derived from two sources; one may have been historical, while the other may have been based on folklore. The former is said to have developed from slaves on Santo Domingo who were chained together by their legs while cutting sugar cane to the beat of a drum, which explains the "dragging leg" aspect of the merengue. The second explanation is based on a story of a great Dominican war hero who suffered a leg wound and gained sympathy from grateful villagers who in turn dragged their legs in solidarity with their injured hero.[9] Ethnomusicologist Paul Austerlitz quotes historian Jean Fouchard, stating that "Mereng evolved from the slave musics such as the chica and calenda with ballroom forms related to French contredanse."[10] The güiro itself was a unifying symbol in the divided Dominican Republic and Haiti; the two slave societies were separated by different colonizers (Spaniards and French), language (Spanish for the Dominican slaves and French for the Haitian slaves), as well divisions by light and dark skin color. However, the güira brought the people together with the sound of merengue music. The French and African slaves of the island used this instrument from African culture and gave themselves a musical platform from which they could express themselves within the confines of slavery.[11] It is possible that Holder gave the güiro to the Tin Man because of his "rusted confinement," which was an allusion to the horrors of enslavement.

Another Afro-Caribbean influence that can be seen in Holder's costumes is in Dorothy's dress, which reflects the *broderie anglaise* style. *Broderie anglaise*, literally translated as "English embroidery," is a "form of whitework embroidery in which round or oval holes are pierced in the material (such as cotton), and the cut edges are then overcast; these holes, or eyelets, are grouped in a pattern that is further delineated by simple embroidery stitches on the surrounding material."[12] Dorothy's white dress, with its red ribbons, lace texture, plunging neckline, and red matching belt, is reminiscent of the *broderie anglaise* dresses popularized in traditional Caribbean creole fashion.[13]

The term creole, however, is an evolving term. Originally, the term was used to describe the "American-born descendants of French and Spanish settlers of Latin America." However, the name became closely associated with the offspring of mixed white and black lineage in antebellum New Orleans, often popularized in music and literature.[14]

The creole dress was a five-part traditional dress called a Madras. The Madras consisted of the poplin blouse, also known as the *chemise decoltée* (a blouse with a scoop neckline). This blouse was decorated with *broderie anglaise*, which consisted of white lace and red ribbons. In addition, the outfit contained an ankle-length skirt decorated with red ribbons. The latter parts of the outfit had a shorter outer skirt consisting of Madras cloth, for which the full ensemble is named, and a triangle-shaped silk scarf.[15]

Holder may have chosen this outfit for Dorothy because it is significant in French West Indian countries such as Martinique, Saint Lucia, and Guadeloupe for its social implications. Most enslaved West Indians were compelled to wear bland, colorless outfits that reinforced their enslavement. These colorless outfits were appropriate for dirty working conditions and reinforced a worker's position as a slave within this society. In contrast, on Sundays, holidays, and feast days, the women donned the colorful Creole madras as a sign of leisure activity and festivity.[16] Perhaps Holder was intentionally making a direct correlation to the drab and gray world of Dorothy's life in Kansas in juxtaposition to her journey to the colorful world of Oz. Holder's bold choice to give Dorothy this costume aligns with the festive nature of her journey to self-discovery and black pride; this may have been a reflection of the French West Indian women who wore their Creole dresses for self-expression in the midst of an oppressive slave society.

African American historical and artistic references play a prominent role in Holder's costumes for *The Wiz*. The Tin Man's armor hinted at the historical legacy of slavery and segregation a great deal. *Smithsonian Magazine* describes the Tin Man's helmet as having been made from a skillet, an allusion to the roles of enslaved African peoples as domestic workers; additionally, "from the Tinman's trash-like armor—beer cans and garbage cans—came echoes of the urban experience."[17] Many African Americans were blue-collar workers, ranging from taxi drivers to bus drivers to factory workers. One 1970s sitcom, *Sanford and Son*, which began its five-year run in 1972, not only promoted the value of urban "junk" but gloried in its abundance. As Fred Sanford, owner of the titular junk shop exclaims: "*Upon this junk I shall build my church*."[18] Like playwright August Wilson, in his epic portrayal of blue-collar workers in his Century Cycle, Holder wanted to draw attention to the beauty of the working black men and women who labored in quiet dignity while the American economy was built on their hard-earned and underappreciated labor. The Tin Man, like Fred Sanford, saw value in the junk of the black experience and found treasure in it, while the larger white culture may have deemed it as trash.

Black activists in the 1970s sought to build upon gains of the civil rights movement. More African Americans were able to make gains in corporate America because of affirmative action policies, school desegregation, and the enforcement of fair housing laws. Sitcoms like *Good Times*, *The Jeffersons*, and *What's Happening* showed blacks in a variety of socioeconomic situations, contexts, and walks of life and showed how they too could be a part of the American Dream. Black athletes such as Julius Erving, Reggie Jackson, and Walter Payton became trailblazers in their respective sports and broke decades-old records along the way. The one black cultural symbol that they all had in common was the Afro hairstyle. The Afro was an enduring symbol of the 1970s, which made social, political, and cultural statements about "Black Pride."

The Afro stood in stark contrast to the chemically processed hairstyles of the 1950s and 1960s, known as "conks." It signaled a return to the "natural" styles of Africa and a rejection of European style of straightened hair. In *The Wiz*, the Cowardly Lion's costume featured a mane that was fashioned after a massive Afro, a far piece from the curly hairstyle of Bert Lahr's Cowardly Lion in the 1939 film à la the flowing locks of England's Charles I. The Cowardly Lion's Afro was not only large in circumference but long as well. In fact, the Afro was nearly a costume in and of itself, skillfully used for both comedic effect in appearance and a cultural statement of blackness in its size. Holder's costume design using the Afro hinted at the Black Power movement as well as the influence of the Black Arts movement, a cultural and artistic revolution that grew out of the Black Power movement. Poets Amiri Baraka, Sonia Sanchez, Don L. Lee, and the musical group The Last Poets asserted their voices with expressions of "black is beautiful," while simultaneously critiquing the white power structure's exploitation of the black community. Instead of representing the King of the Jungle like Lahr's King Charles, Holder fashions *The Wiz's* Cowardly Lion as a king in the mold of Shaka Zulu, the great African chieftain who went to war with the British in South Africa, and some of the great African American leaders such as Martin Luther King Jr. and Malcolm X, who spoke out virulently against oppression. By giving the Cowardly Lion this large Afro, Holder made him a symbol of black pride and African royalty.

Holder's design for the Scarecrow's costume reflected an urban 1970s disco style. His outfit consisted of a large, bright orange and white "apple" hat that was popular in African American culture at the time, with young African American men specifically; a gray and white plaid suit, reminiscent of the leisure suits that were made popular during the disco era by artists such as Barry White and the Isley Brothers; flare-out bell-bottom pants; and platform shoes; along with straw trim around his collar, sleeves, and the bottoms of his pants legs. The Scarecrow could have easily fit in as a Soul Train dancer locking down a Soul Train line on Saturday morning television or a nocturnal denizen boogying down at Studio 54.

Although the disco era was introduced to mainstream America through the groundbreaking film *Saturday Night Fever*, it originated as an underground movement. More importantly, disco provided a haven for self-expression for three marginalized groups: gays, Hispanics, and African Americans. All three groups found their niche and a place of social acceptance at the discotheque because it offered them a place of respite from criticism and an oasis of heterogeneity.[19] The flamboyant and bright clothes alluded to in the Scarecrow's costume were a hallmark of the disco era, which sought to create its own counterculture through upbeat music, acceptance of non-normative lifestyles and gaudy clothing styles, and a rejection of mainstream traditions and styles. The Scarecrow, who no longer wants to be defined by his critics, the Crows, may want to step down from his perch to experience life with his newfound friend Dorothy. The Scarecrow's flamboyant clothing stands out in the field but seems to blend into the Yellow Brick Road ahead of him as he starts on his journey with a self-assured Dorothy at his side.

Perhaps Holder was ahead of his time, but many of his costumes demonstrated a penchant for Afrofuturistic allusions and motifs. In addition to some of the gaudy clothing styles we have seen in the African American references of Holder's disco-themed costumes, there are Afrofuturistic influences in his costumes for *The Wiz* as well. Afrofuturism is a relatively new genre, but it has quickly made a huge impact on arts and culture. While black science fiction has been around for over 100 years, it has only gained mainstream prominence since 1992. It was cultural arts critic Mark Dery, in an essay titled "Black to the Future," who dubbed the genre "Afrofuturism."[20] In Ytasha Womack's book *Afrofuturism: The World of Black Sci-Fi and Fantasy Culture*, art curator and Afrofuturist Ingrid LaFleur defines Afrofuturism as "an intersection of imagination, technology, the future, and liberation. 'I generally define Afrofuturism as a way of imagining possible futures through a black cultural lens.'"[21] Afrofuturism has its roots in the early writings of Charles W. Chestnutt's slave science fiction short story "The Goophered Grapevine," W. E. B. Du Bois's apocalyptic "The Comet," the intergalactic jazz stylings of Sun Ra's "Space Is the Place," and, in recent years, the science-fiction short stories and novels by Samuel R. Delany, the author of "Aye, and Gomorrah," and Octavia Butler, the author of *Kindred*. The genre of Afrofuturism dares to inject black culture, black ideas, black cosmology, and black politics into the future, where it seems that black people are either woefully absent or scarce at best. Not only does Afrofuturism address the need for more Lt. Uhuras of *Star Trek* or Finns of *Star Wars*, but it creates whole black universes that speak to many current issues plaguing the black community today. In Harvard law professor Derrick Bell's short story "The Space Traders," aliens arrive to barter with the United States government to purchase its black citizens in return for clean fuel sources, antipollutants, and monetary wealth. Bell's thesis reflects the echoes of slavery and the harshness of late eighteenth- and early nineteenth-century American policies that encouraged the deportation of blacks to the newly created American colony of Liberia because they were not considered legal citizens of the United States.[22] The story speaks to the perpetual alienation African Americans have endured since the inception of this country and their helplessness without laws in place to secure their rights.

The Wiz's costume resembled that of an astronaut, an alien, or one of the many personalities represented by funkmaster George Clinton's Parliament Funkadelic universe. Parliament Funkadelic created a series of personas that he and his fellow Funkateers acted out during their musical performances. Some of Clinton's incarnations included Dr. Funkenstein, Sir Nose D'VoidofFunk, Starchild, the Brides of Funkenstein, Bootsy and his Rubber Band, Rumpofsteelskin, and the Clones of Funk.[23] Holder may have taken advantage of the group's popularity with black audiences and tapped into the theatricality of Parliament-Funkadelic performances. Like Clinton's musical alter ego Dr. Funkenstein, the Wiz was dressed in an all-white jumpsuit, replete with bell-bottom pants and white platform shoes. Although he sported a rather large Afro like the Cowardly Lion, his Afro had white stripes and he donned what looked like an African mask. His costume reflected the outré nature of the 1970s. Although the Wiz appears to be a menacing, malevolent autocrat, by lording over others he too is searching for his black cultural identity. The Wiz may be a futuristic prototype of authoritarian African leadership, a dire warning that unity cannot be achieved through dictatorship, but only through the principle of *ujima*, collective work and responsibility.[24]

The costumes of both Evillene, the Evil Witch of the West, and the Flying Monkeys also had a futuristic look. However, their look was extremely dystopian and malevolent. While the Wiz feigned malevolence toward the people of Oz with his faux pyrotechnics, Evillene, along with the Flying Monkeys, struck terror in their hearts. Holder put Evillene in a dark blue dress, accessorized her with colorful bangles, gave her a white crown on her forehead, and large braids. Her makeup resembled an African totem, and two large pupils placed on her brassiere functioned as all-watching eyes. Since L. Frank Baum modeled the Flying Monkeys on Native Americans of the Old West, Holder gave them minimalist clothing, which consisted of black fur midriff shirts, black shorts, and a pallid white mask with gaping eyes, and he allowed them to be barefoot to indicate their uncivilized and savage nature.

Many of us may be familiar with Geoffrey Holder through films such as *Live and Let Die*, in which he played the villainous Baron Samedi; *Boomerang*, as the sex-crazed TV commercial director Nelson; or from television commercials as the cool West Indian "mahn" who asked, "Don't you feel good about . . . ah, ah, ah . . . 7Up?" and declared the soft drink the

"UnCola." Holder was also an accomplished dancer with the Alvin Ailey American Dance Theatre, and he appeared in such seminal theatrical productions as Truman Capote's Caribbean-themed musical *House of Flowers*, played Lucky in Samuel Beckett's *Waiting for Godot*, and starred in a modern reworking of Shakespeare's *Othello*. Holder brought a wealth of his own performance experience and artistic sensibility to bear when he was chosen to take over direction of *The Wiz* at such a pivotal time in its production. Holder once remarked of his philosophy of life and art: "All I can give you is my truth, whether you like it or not. When I in look into a mirror, I see God. I may be in his image. He may have big lips just like me."[25] His truth was one that desired to show the beauty of black culture in many artistic settings, whether it was visual art, dance, theatre or film. Geoffrey Holder's genius shone brightly not only in his direction of *The Wiz* but in the intentionality of his costumes to reflect various aspects of the African Diaspora. His innovative costumes will long serve as a template for those who design costumes to enhance the characters of a show while sending cultural messages in the process.

Notes

1. Jeremy Aufderheide, "How the Wiz Was," Lulu.com, 2014, 61–62.

2. Brynn Cox, "Vintage *Playbill*: The Wiz, 1974," *Playbill*, January 5, 2013, http://www.playbill.com/article/vintage-playbill-the-wiz-1974-com-201224.

3. Aufderheide, "How the Wiz Was," 73.

4. "The Wiz," Internet Broadway Database, https://www.ibdb.com/broadway-production/the-wiz-3716, accessed February 18, 2018.

5. Cox, "Vintage *Playbill*: The Wiz, 1974."

6. Janell Hobson, "Middle Passages: Gendered Diasporas: The Musical Heritage of the African Diaspora," University at Albany, State University of New York, http://www.albany.edu/faculty/jhobson/middle_passages/musical_memory.html. This website was created to accompany a 2015 art exhibit titled "Baggage Claim: An Art Exhibit," which focused on the "invisible luggage in the form of memories, language, culture, and skills" brought from Africa by enslaved peoples.

7. "Glossary of Terms Relating to Afro-Caribbean Music," *Smithsonian Latino Center*, 2005, http://latino.si.edu/virtualgallery/Sabor/SalsaResearchResources/SonClaveLounge/SalsaGlossary.htm.

8. John M. Schechter, James Blade, and James Holland, "Guiro," *The New Grove Dictionary of Jazz*, 2nd ed.; quoted in *Oxford Music Online*, http://www.oxfordmusiconline.com/subscriber/article/grove/music/12008?q=guiro&search=quick&source=omo_gmo&pos=1&_start=1#firsthit.

9. Luis Alba, "Tracing the Origins of Salsa Music," *Smithsonian Latino Center*, 2002, http://latino.si.edu/virtualgallery/sabor/SalsaResearchResources/articles/The%20History%20of%20Salsa%20Dancing2.htm.

10. Paul Austerlitz, *Merengue: Dominican Music and Dominican Identity* (Philadelphia: Temple University Press, 1997), 2.

11. Ibid, 3.

12. "Broderie Anglaise," *Encyclopedia Britannica*, May 27, 1999, https://www.britannica.com/art/broderie-anglaise.

13. Katie Knowles, "Ease On Down the Road: A 'Super Soul Musical' Celebrates African American Culture," National Museum of African American History and Culture, 2017, https://nmaahc.si.edu/explore/stories/collection/ease-down-road.

14. James D. Hart, ed., with revisions and additions by Phillip W. Leininger, "Creole," *The Concise Oxford Companion to American Literature*, 1986 (2002), 151, http://www.oxfordreference.com.hssu.idm.oclc.org/view/10.1093/acref/9780195047714.001.0001/acref-9780195047714.

15. "About Saint Lucia: National Dress of Saint Lucia, *Consulate General of Saint Lucia in New York*, http://saintluciaconsulateny.org/about-saint-lucia/.

16. Ibid.

17. Victoria Dawson, "The Tinman's Hat from 'The Wiz' Offers Just a Hint of the Musical's Beating Heart," *Smithsonian*, January 5, 2015, http://www.smithsonianmag.com/smithsonian-institution/tinmans-hat-from-the-wiz-offers-hint-musicals-beating-heart-180953718/.

18. *Sanford and* Son, "The Reverend Sanford," directed by Norman Lear. Season 6, Episode 19 (original air date February 11, 1977), http://www.imdb.com/title/tt0694166/quotes, accessed February 21, 2018.

19. Richard Powers, "Brief Histories of Social Dance: The Disco Lifestyle," *Stanford University Dance Division*, n.d., https://socialdance.stanford.edu/Syllabi/disco_lifestyle.htm.

20. Mark Dery, "Black to the Future," *Flame Wars: The Discourse of Cyberculture* (Durham, NC: Duke University Press, 1994), 180.

21. Ytasha Womack, *Afrofuturism: The World of Black Sci-Fi and Fantasy Culture* (Chicago: Lawrence Hill Books, 2013), 9.

22. Derrick Bell, "The Space Traders," *Faces at the Bottom of the Well* (New York: HarperCollins, 1992), 159–94, http://liberalarts.iupui.edu/mpsg/Essays/Bell%20-%20The%20Space%20Traders.pdf.

23. "Funkateerz," *Funkcyclopedia*, n.d., https://web.archive.org/web/20070306205437/http://www.georgeclinton.com/htmlversion/gc/funkateer_funkcyclopedia.htm.

24. "Kwanzaa: A Celebration of Family, Community, and Culture: The Seven Principles," *Official Kwanzaa Website*, n.d., http://www.officialkwanzaawebsite.org/7principles.shtml.

25. Camille O. Cosby and Howard L. Bingham, eds., *A Wealth of Wisdom: Legendary African American Elders Speak* (New York: Washington Square Press, 2004), 188.

"On the [Historical] Sublime"

J. R. Planché's *King John* and the
Romantic Ideal of the Past

Andrew Gibb

THE 1823 COVENT GARDEN production of *King John*, which featured costumes designed by James Robinson (J. R.) Planché, is often credited with the first systematic deployment of historically accurate costuming. For many years, theatre historians treated this notable moment in design as one of many steps in a seemingly centuries-long march toward progressively greater stage realism. The extent to which this interpretation held sway is evidenced by the fact that historians customarily linked Planché's antiquarianism to the earlier practices of *habit à la romaine*, local color, and eastern exoticism, as well as to eighteenth-century spectacles such as David Garrick's Elizabethan-dressed Shakespearean tragedies and Macklin's 1741 Shylock.[1]

The problem with such an understanding of *King John* lay in its progressivist stance. It relied upon an assumption that historical accuracy in stage effects was an inevitable standard, one that slowly but surely evolved over time. But while the earlier practices noted heretofore certainly contributed to an artistic trajectory that allowed for a new way of representing history onstage, they neither individually nor collectively provided a satisfactory explanation of why artists and audiences should have chosen 1823 as *the* moment to enthusiastically embrace historically accurate costuming.

To my mind, the answer to that question cannot be located in the spectacular innovations of Planché's costumes themselves, although they were undoubtedly something new and exciting. Ultimately, there was something far more profound about the experience of *King John* than that of an audience recognizing the genius of a designer. What was happening in the space of the Convent Garden theatre was that a group of early nineteenth-century Londoners, through the medium of theatre (or more specifically, theatrical costuming), *were* talking to each other about history in a new way. Given my interpretation of the event, this essay reveals little that is new about the facts of the 1823 Covent Garden production. Instead, with it I seek to tell the origin story of a particular theatrical convention, that of historically accurate costuming. For this reason, in the pages that follow, I engage far more deeply with the context of period events and philosophies than with the archival details of Planché's costumes.[2] One could say that my primary interest with this essay is not the particulars of *King John* as a historical production, but rather the historical embeddedness of *King John*'s costuming practices.

For some time now, historians have been steadily moving away from presentist and progressivist explanations of past theatrical practice, and with respect to *King John*, the old characterization of Planché's choices as a kind of budding realism has largely been supplanted by interpretations that privilege social contexts over aesthetic ones. Most compellingly, theatre historians have tied the nineteenth-century desire for historical accuracy in costuming to rising nationalist sentiment among period audiences, an argument convincingly made by Richard Schoch, and echoed by the authors of the next-generation *Theatre Histories* textbook.[3]

There is, however, a notable discrepancy between Schoch's study and the treatment of *King John* by McConachie et al. The latter authors see nationalism at work in the success of the 1823 production, while Schoch, though prominently mentioning Planché, nevertheless takes as his primary exemplars the productions staged by Charles Kean in the 1850s, a generation after Planché's innovation. Why should Kean's stagings prove to be a more fitting example of theatrical nationalism than Kemble's? Interestingly, the lag between Kemble and those who followed was noted by Oscar Brockett as early as 1968, when he wrote: "In spite of the success of these productions, Kemble did not repeat the experiment until 1827, and it was not until Macready accepted it in 1837 that authenticity was consistently exploited. Thus, while Planché's work in 1823 must be considered a landmark, it did not bring an immediate revolution in theatrical practice."[4] What can account for the delay between Planché's 1823 innovation and its full adoption at mid-century?

While I would judge as sound the connection between the popularity of historically accurate costuming and the emerging ideology of nationalism, I nevertheless contend that such a link was forged in stages, and in collaboration with audiences. Before theatregoing Englishmen could embrace historical accuracy as an expression of their unique national past, they needed first to cultivate an understanding of the past as a time fundamentally different from their own.[5] Theatrical costuming conventions before the early nineteenth century demonstrated no real concern for the historical specificity of characters and settings. The fact that producers and audiences fully accepted those conventions indicates that their sense of the past was fundamentally different than that held by the costumers and audiences of today. More to the point, in order for Garrick's audiences of the late eighteenth century to be transformed into Kean's fervently nationalist spectators of the mid-nineteenth, their notion of the past as an undifferentiated prologue to the present must at some point have been shattered, and replaced with a sense of history as a time apart.

Such a sense of distanciation was a key component of Romantic philosophies of history, which arose in no small part as a response to the traumatic experiences of the Napoleonic Wars. Drawing upon recent scholarly interpretations of Romantic historiography, I argue here that the success of Planché's *King John* in 1823 represented a successful activation the "historical sublime."

As theorized by historians of Romantic-era thought, the historical sublime parallels the notion of the aesthetic sublime advanced by Romantic philosophers and artists, among them theatre theorist and playwright Friedrich Schiller. What links the aesthetic and historical sublime is a reliance upon the contemplation of an unbridgeable gulf between the Real and the Ideal. For those Romantics whose realm was artistic expression, that gulf was often situated between the self and the world, the latter often represented by the incomprehensible grandeur of nature (as evidenced in Romantic painting, for instance). For Romantic historians and their readers, who had lived through the horrors of the recent Napoleonic Wars, the unbridgeable gulf of the historical sublime was the one that separated them from a pre-Napoleonic, pre-Revolutionary world, one that had been shaped by residual medieval and Renaissance neoclassical ideas about human nature. For Romantic theatre audiences, I will argue, the historical sublime was enacted when they were presented with visions of that unattainable past, a past that present shocks had suddenly made sublimely remote from their own lives.

On October 29, 1823, playbills began appearing in London advertising coming attractions at the Theatre Royal Convent Garden, foremost of which was a production of Shakespeare's *King John*.[6] At first glance, theatre regulars were probably not very much surprised, as the play had been a mainstay of actor-manager Charles Kemble's repertoire since the 1800–1801 season.[7] But those that took a moment to read the advertisement were no doubt intrigued by a prominent teaser: "This present MONDAY, 24th NOVEMBER, 1823, Will be revived, Shakespeare's Tragedy of KING JOHN With an Attention to COSTUME never before equaled on the English Stage. Every Character will appear in the precise HABIT OF THE PERIOD: The whole of the Dresses and Decorations being executed from indisputable authorities, such as Monumental Effigies, Seals, illuminated MSS., &c."[8] Just a few years before, the announcement of a scenic extravaganza at Covent Garden would have been commonplace, as manager Henry Harris had established the venue as the home of "gaudy spectacle and gilded melodramas."[9] But the directorship of the theatre had recently changed hands, and it was experiencing something of a recovery of dignity. New manager Charles Kemble sought to woo a different type of patron with dignified productions of the Bard.

For the benefit of these new playgoers, who might have been leery of the return of vulgar novelty, the playbill advertised that "the Costumes are published, and may be had of J.MILLER, Fleet-street, and all other Booksellers."[10] Anyone inquiring at Mr. Miller's would have found a booklet prepared by designer J. R. Planché, explaining the management's intention to make the "the dresses and decorations of Shakespeare's plays, if possible, worthy of them."[11] Whether such protestations were sincere or calculating (evidence suggests Planché's intentions were the former, while Kemble's may have been the latter), they succeeded in creating just the right mixture of dignity and sensationalism, and the house was packed on opening night.[12] The response was immediate and overwhelming. Planché recalled "a roar of approbation, accompanied by four distinct rounds of applause."[13]

Our knowledge of exactly what the opening night audience so vociferously approved is based upon the costume plates and accompanying notes assembled by Planché and printed by Miller. The twenty-two images depict an array of characters, from leads such as King John and "William, surnamed Longspee or Longsword, Earl of Salisbury," to minor roles like "English Nobleman of the 13th Century" and "English Herald of the 13th Century."[14] Far from the pumpkin breeches of Garrick's eighteenth-century stagings of Shakespeare's tragedies, these costumes feature thirteenth-century period-appropriate silhouettes and accents: gowns and hose, surcoats, cloaks, gloves, baldrics, mail armor, period broadswords, and large shields. What is important to note about these designs is that the feeling of historical accuracy they engendered was conveyed by two distinct yet interrelated phenomena: each individual costume displayed a wealth of historical details and, at the same time, all the costumes (from king to page) received the same antiquarian treatment. Taken together they presented a whole world, separate and distinct from that of 1823 England, in both their particulars and in the aggregate. Such an all-encompassing vision must have been breathtaking to Planché's audience, as their enthusiastic response would suggest.

Kemble's *King John* is not only given credit for the first use of historically accurate costuming; it is also cited as the inspiration for historically accurate representation in all visual elements. Though the producers did not make a parallel effort in scenic design with *King John*, the show's success prompted the management in that direction. The playbill for Kemble's 1831 presentation of *Henry VIII* advertised representations of "St. Paul's and London Bridge, as they were in 1533."[15] Of course, as Brockett, McConachie, and Schoch have made clear, it was not until the later productions of actor-managers William Charles Macready and Charles Kean that historical accuracy would be consistently applied to all elements of production. Nevertheless, the reactions of Kemble's 1823 audiences indicate that something new and extraordinary was afoot.

While the upscale audiences of the Covent Garden were undoubtedly surprised by the spectacle of Planché's costuming, it would not have been their first exposure to the innovations of Romantic art. Historians have cited Edmund Burke's *Inquiry into the Origins of Our Ideas of the Sublime and Beautiful*, published in 1756, as the first manifestation of Romantic ideas in England, and the herald of the Romantic turn in British visual arts.[16] Wordsworth's and Coleridge's *Lyrical Ballads* are credited with heralding the entrance of Romantic thought into English letters in 1798.[17] Walter Scott's *Ivanhoe*, the epitome of the British Romantic historical novel, appeared in print just three years before *King John*'s premiere. Such are the entry points of Romantic aesthetics into English painting, poetry, and fiction. In its usual fashion, theatre seems to have taken longer to adopt the newest artistic innovations. By 1823, *King John*'s audiences would have been used to a steady diet of revolutionary artistic experimentation. That said, of the aforementioned works, only those of Scott and Planché were introduced after the Napoleonic Wars, and I would argue that it is no coincidence that they are the only ones that engage both the aesthetic and the historical sublime.

By whatever standard one chooses to apply, there is little doubt that European art was fully engaged with Romanticism by 1823. Springing from a disillusionment with Enlightenment modes of thought that had dominated the previous century, Romanticism as a school was a constitutionally loose collection of thinkers and artists, making it hard to pin down their movement precisely. What ideas they did share in common tended to keep them apart personally: most Romantics were individualists and nationalists, and both tendencies worked against the free and open exchange of ideas that had characterized the Enlightenment. Nevertheless, despite a lack of cohesion, some cross-germination took place. With respect to Britain, perhaps the most important international connections were made by Samuel Taylor Coleridge, who familiarized himself with the works of the great German philosopher Immanuel Kant, as well as Kant's most notable artistic interpreter, Friedrich Schiller.

In his *Critique of Pure Reason*, first published in 1781, Kant postulated an essential separation of the world from the individual, a distinction that established a paradigm of dualism common to almost all subsequent Romantic thought. Kant's formulation of the Romantic concept of the "sublime" proceeded directly from this split. For Kant, the sublime is a transcendent state that can be realized only by a willful denial of the physical world, a denial that secures release from the constraints of material existence.

Kant did not conceive of the sublime as a state that could be artistically inspired. His disciple Friedrich Schiller, however, was convinced that sublimity could be achieved through art. In the essays "On the Pathetic" (1793) and "On the Sublime" (1801), Schiller attempted to theorize a place for the arts in a Romantic worldview. Dramatic representation, at least of the tragic variety, could provide an aesthetic pleasure through the contemplation of the disharmony and tension between the world and the individual. This could be accomplished by representing a character who, when left with no choice by the world of the senses, refuses to obey the dictates of that world. Such a choice to deny the sensuous world usually resulted in the hero's death, but such punishment had lost its power to harm, for the hero had obtained the sublime. Initially, Schiller held that aesthetic enjoyment arose solely from our contemplation of the hero's sublimity. But in his "On the Use of the Chorus in the Tragedy" (1803), written near the end of his life, he expressed his belief that viewing such sublimity could enable an audience to achieve their own.[18]

As a man whose lifetime straddled both the Enlightenment and Romantic periods, Schiller's intellectual labor reflected the learned preoccupations of both. In addition to working as a dramatist and critic (both occupations typical of an Enlightenment gentleman), he also wrote histories, a preferred genre of Romantic writers (especially German ones). While Schiller's theorizations only touched upon the aesthetic manifestations of the sublime, his interest in history (and particularly his historical plays) make him an appropriate bridge to a discussion of the historical sublime.

The Romantic era saw a new engagement with history, brought about by several factors, including the great archeological excavations of the eighteenth century, which sparked a wave of antiquarian collecting. But the most profound influence on contemporary ideas about what had come before was not these tantalizing glimpses of a wondrous past, but rather the overabundant evidence of a violent present. In 1789, France imploded, setting a new standard for revolutionary bloodletting. In 1798, French armies forged in the crucible of civil war exploded across the map of Europe. Nearly twenty years of general war followed, snuffing out countless lives and the spark of optimism that had inspired European culture since the Renaissance. Aftershocks spread across Europe following the fighting, even in victorious Britain, where decades of unresolved economic and social problems resurfaced in distressing, sometimes violent forms.[19] Any ideal vision that survived into the Romantic period had become an unobtainable goal, a state that could at best be approximated today and despairingly hoped for tomorrow. By contrast, the Past (with its newly acquired mental capital "P"), a time now distantly seen through the haze of terrible memories and current anxieties, retained the charm of the idyllic, and to it the postwar generation turned with a newfound veneration.[20]

The universalist and progressivist assumptions of Enlightenment history were dashed by the tumultuous political events at the turn of the nineteenth century. Among the results of the failure of Reason were a profound sense of the world's inexplicability, as heralded by Kant, and the rise of contentious nationalisms, as inspired by Bonaparte. The society that arose from these new conditions had new uses for history, new truths it needed to illustrate by historical example. Appropriately enough, the favored subject of historians became the one deemed most unworthy of Enlightenment historiography: the Middle Ages. Despised by the French *philosophes* as an age of barbarism, the medieval era was seen by German Romantics as the font of a national ethos. Instead of seeking a universal progression of history stretching back to ancient times, German historians focused on the uniqueness of the German experience, the essence of their *volk*. Inspired by a reaction to Napoleonic hegemony, this emphasis on national (and "racial") exceptionalism would provide the ideological fuel for the eventual unification of Germany in 1871. Across the English Channel, Britain, another imperial power rising from the ashes of Napoleon's ambitions, also looked to the Middle Ages for proof of an ancient pedigree. The newfound fascination with the medieval in the British Isles extended beyond the dry histories of academics; it sold best in the form of Sir Walter Scott's fictional tales of knightly adventure.[21]

All these histories, whether British or German, scholarly or fictional, shared something else besides their nationalism: an ideal separation of the past from the present. Enlightenment thinkers saw history as a progression, contemplation of which merely served to help explain the enlightened present. For the Romantics, the Past became a location of the Ideal, and contemplation of its irretrievable separation from the present could generate a sense of the sublime similar in nature to the artistic sublime enunciated by Schiller. Although the historians and artists of the period did not speak of their work in such terms, twenty-first century historiographers and critics have noted such a treatment of the past in the period's writing, a mode that has been labeled the "historical sublime."[22]

The concept of the historical sublime is defined by historian Ann Rigney as an "evocation of the limits of our historical understanding . . . stimulat[ing] the imagination of readers to reflect upon what lies beyond their purview."[23] In other words, when the individual is confronted with the utter and awesome unknowability of the past, he can enjoy a feeling of the sublime similar to that experienced by Schiller's theatre audiences.

Historical sublimity, like Schiller's artistic version, relies upon a separation: a gap between the known and the unknowable. In order for that gap to have its intended effect, attention must be drawn to it. As Rigney notes, "The aesthetic effect . . . involves focusing the attention of the reader on the nature of the historical representation as much as on the positive information given about the past."[24] Here we see that, for Rigney, the historical sublime is an experience of history that is fundamentally aesthetic. Crossing the bridge she builds for us, we can begin to understand an artistic event like the production of *King John* as a simultaneous expression of both Romantic aesthetic ideals and the Romantic view of history; in other words, as an example of the historical sublime at work in art. She furthers the connection between the two sublimes by emphasizing how the aesthetic enjoyment of the historical sublime is dependent upon drawing the attention of the onlooker to the gap between reality and representation. Thus the importance of the sources cited in Kemble's playbills and the images provided in Planché's booklet: the pleasure of the historical sublime can only be activated when we understand how limited is our knowledge of the past. For this reason, Rigney dubs the historical sublime "the Pleasure of Ignorance."[25]

It follows, then, that the greater our acknowledged ignorance of the past, the more pleasure we experience in contemplating it. And our knowledge of our own ignorance is conversely related to how much we *do* know. Perhaps counterintuitively, the more detail we are given by the historian (or in the case of *King John*, the costumer), the more we become aware of all the things we don't know; how foreign the past really is. Our sense of our own ignorance then activates the historical sublime. This explains Planché's extraordinary attention to detail with *King John*: complete head-to-toe representations, extending from the king's crown to the lowliest page's boots. Inundating his spectators with a visual cornucopia of strange sartorial differences (peculiarities that the playbill guaranteed to be absolutely correct), through a spectacle played out across the canvasses of each and every body onstage, Planché opened his audiences' awareness to the great Romantic gulf that separated them from their Ideal Past. The addition of scenic elements in later productions only added to the effect. In the matter of historically accurate costuming and scenic design, more knowledge equals less knowledge, which leads to more sublimity.

The length to which the historian (or the artist) has gone in the attempt to represent the past only adds to our pleasurable ignorance. Rigney writes, "The more historians meet the resistance of their material by going as far as they can into its complexity . . . the greater the aesthetic appeal of the work."[26] With Planché's designs, we can see this dynamic in action. The original playbills that mentioned the costumes went beyond citing the types of sources consulted. Lower down the bill, underneath the actors' names, the potential audience member was treated to a detailed listing of those sources:

> Authorities for the Costume
> KING JOHN'S EFFIGY, in Worcester Cathedral, and His Great Seals.
> QUEEN ELINOR'S EFFIGY, In the Abbey of Fonteveraud.
> EFFIGY of the EARL of SALISBURY, in Salisbury Cathedral.
> EFFIGY of the EARL of PEMBROKE, in the Temple Church, London.
> KING JOHN'S SILVER CUP, in the possession of the Corporation of
> King's Lynn, Norfolk.
> ILLUMINATED MSS., in the British Museum, Bodleian and Bennet
> College Libraries, and the Works of Camden, Montfaucon, Sandford, Strutt,
> Gough, Stothard, Meyrick, &c.[27]

Such a density of information serves as a visual representation of the monumentally endless layers of history separating the reader from the reality that can be but poorly represented on the Covent Garden stage. Additionally, the preponderance of effigies on the list might be read as a direct reminder of death, which, though separating us from our past, may in some way be momentarily and sublimely overcome during this performance.

Given my heavy reliance upon the playbill to make my point, it is critical to note that the imaginative promise of this advertisement did not entirely match the actuality of Planché's finished costumes. For his 1968 essay "The Costume Designs of James Robinson Planché," Paul Reinhardt completed an extensive comparison of Planché's historical costume with the sources the designer was known to have consulted. The results indicate that Planché may have been less devoted to historical accuracy than has been assumed by theatre historians such as myself.[28]

In the text of the playbill, effigies and illuminated manuscripts—both physical artifacts of the historical period to be represented—are given top billing. At the very bottom of the list are cited a number of secondary sources, the work of scholars long removed from the thirteenth century, and thus perhaps somewhat less sublime. Two of the final four, Joseph Strutt's *Complete View of the Dress and Habits of the People of England* (1796–1799) and C. A. Stothard's *The Monumental Effigies of Great Britain* (1811), are identified by Reinhardt as the source of "over half" of Planché's *King John* designs. A reliance on these secondary sources does not of course signal an unwillingness by Planché to produce the most accurate costumes (they were, after all, the most cutting-edge scholarship of their day). But their far less prominent location on the playbill (a document one assumes Planché had a hand in composing, given that they were in effect the footnotes to his research) seems to acknowledge their lesser potential for summoning the mystery of the past.

Even more damning is Reinhardt's discovery that Planché played fast and loose with his sources. "Of the designs which can be compared with the sources from which they were taken," writes Reinhardt, "not one is exactly like the original source."[29] Looking into these discrepancies, the scholar offers informed conjecture regarding Plaché's reasons: "For several costumes he removes items which cover the face, presumably to make faces visible and voices audible. The introduction of buttons to fasten garments may have been either for function or for realism. Enlargement of details would make them more visible in a large theatre."[30] Most revealing of all is a direct quote from Planché, referring to the costume of the English Herald. Planché wrote that the coif displayed in the original source for that costume had to be removed, because it "would be anything but picturesque upon the stage."[31] Such a comment, as well as the reasonable assumptions advanced by Reinhardt regarding other choices, would seem to indicate that Planché was not actively seeking the kind of historical sublime that I hypothesize here.

In light of such revelations, my reliance upon the playbill becomes all the more important to my argument. The generation of a feeling of the historical sublime may or may not have been the conscious (or unconscious) intent of Planché, Kemble, and the other actors who wore the innovative costuming. But if the historical sublime was activated in the Covent Garden theatre on that November night in 1823, it would have been a phenomenon experienced by the audience. And the knowledge required to summon that audience's pleasurable ignorance did not come from their knowledge of Planché's production process, but from their reading of the playbill, and possibly from the booklet of published designs available at the bookseller's. Those documents summoned the authority of the designer's sources (especially the primary ones) but did not reproduce them for the scrutiny of the reader. Planché's audiences were only aware of what they were told, that what they were seeing onstage was an authoritatively established reconstruction of English life some six centuries before they were born. However misguided they may have been, they had the knowledge they needed to summon a sublime experience. Thus it was Planché's advertising, not his practical theatrical decisions, that is the key to understanding the effect his costumes had.

If we are to accept that the later English audiences of the 1850s enjoyed Charles Kean's costume dramas as patriotic retellings of their national origin stories, then they must have conceived of what they saw onstage as not only quintessentially English, but also historically removed from their own modern experience. The detail and completeness of Planché's costumes awakened the audience's awareness of the gulf between their own time and the past. As the figures of England's past withdrew across that chasm, they took on the mold of mythic, originary heroes, against whose example the citizenry of an ascendant nation could measure themselves (in the case of *King John*, of course, the mantle for heroism would have to be carried by Faulconbridge, as John was far from a sympathetic titular character). The opening of that Romantic gap required the kind of detail that only an antiquarian like Planché could provide, introducing the spectator to his or her own ignorance, and in the process activating the historical sublime. Once Kemble had introduced his audiences to the pleasures of historical ignorance, Macready, Kean, and others could make later use of this new mode of historical representation for patriotic (and commercial) uses.

By Kean's day, the extension of historical accuracy to scenic elements furthered the spectator's access to the historical sublime by eliminating historical gaps within the *mise-en-scène*, increasing knowledge and thus pleasurable ignorance. The coming of film at the end of the century provided whole new possibilities, not only through epic increases in scale from the contained frame of the proscenium to the panoramic possibilities of the camera lens, but also thanks to the now literally unbridgeable chasm between the real life taking place in the auditorium and the imaginary world of the cinematic diegesis. The advent of computer-generated imagery eliminated traditional budgetary limits upon the scale of scenic representation, making it possible for audiences to contemplate their irretrievable distance from the games of ancient Rome (*Gladiator*, 2000), the human sacrifices of the Maya (*Apocalyto*, 2006), even the Napoleonic sea battles that some of Planché's spectators may have witnessed firsthand (*Master and Commander*, 2003). All three of these filmic examples, however, point to an important distinction between the 1823 audiences of *King John* and present-day moviegoers, one that is anchored in divergent popular attitudes about history. For today's media consumers, the spectacular Past no longer appears to elicit desire for an unattainable

Romantic Ideal. Instead, we seem to watch in order to celebrate our safe separation from a violent, barbaric history. Patriotic films such as *Saving Private Ryan* (1998) may be an exception to this rule, and in this respect it is worth noting a parallel: like that World War II epic, *King John* is filled with battles and other forms of violent death. Perhaps in the case of nationalist expressions, the historical sublime continues to offer us pleasure. And yet, the recent film that appears to have come closest to inspiring something like Romantic sublimity in its audiences is *Avatar* (2009), a film that is widely reported to have driven some spectators to thoughts of suicide when contemplating the unattainability of its fictional world, Pandora.[32] In this case, the filmmakers appear to have succeeded in fostering what might be labeled a "future sublime."[33]

That twenty-first century audiences might find this new aesthetic experience far more emotionally gripping than that of the historical sublime speaks volumes about the difference between Romantic and Postmodern attitudes about the past. Indeed, one might argue that the cataclysms of the twentieth century have led Western society to once again conceive of history as an obstacle to be overcome, thus returning us full circle to the attitudes of the Enlightenment.

Notes

1. In the first edition of Oscar Brockett's *History of the Theatre* (Boston: Allyn and Bacon, 1968), mention of *King John* appears under "Theatrical Conditions, 1790–1843," part of the chapter about "English Theatre in the 19th Century" (at 443). This section is preceded by "Costume Practices, 1660–1790" in "The English Theatre, 1642–1790" (280–82), and "Costume Practices" in "Italy and France in the 18th Century" (324–27), segments that both highlight the earlier practices. My thanks to Simon Williams and Diane Holley, whose teaching inspired this essay, and whose advice improved it greatly. Also to Xiaoyan Deng, whose labor rescued it from oblivion.

2. For readers who may wish a more complete catalogue of those details than is provided by my summary, a number of excellent studies have been published, most notably Paul Reinhardt, "The Costume Designs of James Robinson Planché (1796–1880)," *Educational Theatre Journal* 20, no. 4 (1968): 524–44, upon which I have relied heavily for this essay. Reinhardt's study is replete with images of Planché's designs, in many cases laid side-by-side with the historical artworks upon which they were based.

3. See Richard Schoch, *Shakespeare's Victorian Stage: Performing History in the Theatre of Charles Kean* (Cambridge: Cambridge University Press, 1998), and Bruce McConachie, Tobin Nellhaus, Carol Fisher Sorgenfrei, and Tamara Underiners, *Theatre Histories: An Introduction*, 3rd ed. (New York: Routledge, 2016), 304.

4. Brockett, *History of the Theatre*, 443.

5. This modern understanding of history as a time apart, and its relatively recent emergence, is treated most notably in David Lowenthal, *The Past Is a Foreign Country* (Cambridge: Cambridge University Press, 1985).

6. Evelyn B. Richmond, "Historical Costuming: A Footnote," *Shakespeare Quarterly* 11 (1960): 233–34, at 234.

7. Jane Williamson, *Charles Kemble, Man of the Theatre* (Lincoln: University of Nebraska Press, 1964), 118.

8. Quoted in Richmond, "Historical Costuming," 233.

9. Williamson, *Charles Kemble*, 145.

10. Quoted in Richmond, "Historical Costuming," 233.

11. Quoted in Williamson, *Charles Kemble*, 167.

12. In his memoirs, Planché recalled the "casual conversation" between himself and Kemble that led to the *King John* costumes, during which he argued at length for the "propriety" of historically accurate costuming. According to the antiquarian, "Mr. Kemble admitted the fact, and perceived the pecuniary advantage that might result from the experiment." Planché, *The Recollections and Reflections of J. R. Planché (Somerset Herald): A Professional Autobiography* (London: Tinsley Brothers, 1872), 53.

13. Quoted in Williamson, *Charles Kemble*, 167.

14. Images reproduced in Reinhardt, "The Costume Designs."

15. Ibid., 168.

16. Alicia Finkel, *Romantic Stages: Set and Costume Design in Victorian England* (Jefferson, NC: McFarland and Company, 1996), 3.

17. John Blades, "Introduction," *Wordworth and Coleridge: Lyrical Ballads* (New York: Palgrave Macmillian, 2004), 3.

18. My understanding of Schiller's and Kant's ideas about the sublime and art derives in large part from Marvin Carlson's treatment of them in his *Theories of the Theatre: A Historical and Critical Survey, from the Greeks to the Present* (Ithaca, NY: Cornell University Press, 1984), 175–77.

19. An excellent summary of these postwar social upheavals, including the violent clashes at the Spa Fields, Peterloo, and Queen Caroline's funeral, can be found in Norman McCord and Bill Purdue, *British History, 1815–1914*, 2nd ed. (Oxford: Oxford University Press, 2007), 22–32.

20. Lowenthal, *The Past Is a Foreign Country*, 96.

21. The brief account of Enlightenment and Romantic history I have included here is largely informed by Lowenthal's work, as well as Michael Bentley, *Modern Historiography: An Introduction* (London: Routledge, 1999).

22. Ann Rigney, *Imperfect Histories: The Elusive Past and the Legacy of Romantic Historicism* (Ithaca, NY: Cornell University Press, 2001).

23. Ibid., 114.

24. Ibid.

25. Ibid., 113.

26. Ibid., 114–15.

27. Richmond, "Historical Costuming," 233.

28. Reinhardt, "The Costume Designs of James Robinson Planché."

29. Ibid., 529.

30. Ibid., 539.

31. Quoted ibid., 539.

32. "The Avatar Effect: Movie-goers Feel Depressed and Suicidal at Not Being Able to Visit Utopian Alien Planet," *Daily Mail,* January 12, 2010, http://www.dailymail.co.uk/news/article-1242409/The-Avatar-effect-Movie-goers -feel-depressed-suicidal-able-visit-utopian-alien-planet.html.

33. Film scholar Todd McGowan writes of a future sublime, calling it "the only form of sublime that exists in the capitalist universe" (*Capitalism and Desire: The Psychic Cost of Free Markets* [New York: Columbia University Press, 2016], 228). Incidentally, the makers of *Avatar* also appear to have solved what had always been the greatest challenge to the historical sublime: the irrepressible present of the actor's live body (or in the case of film, the unmistakable body of the familiar star). This reconciliation was accomplished by replacing the live or filmed body with a computer-assisted morph of actor and costume, a feat of technological wizardry that may well eventually lead to a wholesale redefinition of our notions of costuming.

Contributors

Aly Renee Amidei is the assistant professor of costume design at the University of North Carolina, Charlotte. She has also worked as a designer and playwright in Chicago for the last sixteen years, where she is an ensemble member of both Strawdog Theatre Company and Lifeline Theatre and a founding member and former artistic director of the horror theatre company WildClaw. Her costume and makeup designs have been seen at Michigan Shakespeare Festival, Irish Theater of Chicago, Buffalo Theater Ensemble, Stage Left, Artistic Home, House Theater of Chicago, Piven Workshop, Pittsburgh Irish and Classical Theatre, and Vitalist Theater. Her creative research focus concerns the role of the "designer as dramaturg." She practices this research by designing new works or reenvisioning extant texts through the concept of "world-building" and a design process that mirrors common dramaturgy protocols: analysis, research, problem solving, practical application, and reflection. Aly received her BA in Theatre from Knox College, an MFA in Costume Design from Carnegie Mellon University, and a Certificate in Fashion Design from the College of Dupage.

Gregory S. Carr is an instructor of speech and theatre at Harris-Stowe State University. He is an accomplished director and playwright. Two of his plays, *Johnnie Taylor Is Gone* and *A Colored Funeral*, have been given productions at the historic Karamu House in Cleveland. His essay "Top Brass: Theatricality, Themes, and Theology in James Weldon Johnson's *God's Trombones*" appeared in *Theatre Symposium 21: Ritual, Religion and Theatre*. Gregory's play *Tinderbox* received a staged reading at the East St. Louis 1917 Centennial Commission and Cultural Initiative Academic Conference. His essay "The Miracle on 23rd: Examining the Vitality of the St. Louis Black Repertory as One of the Premier Black Theatres of the 21st Century" appears in the *Routledge Companion to African American Theatre*.

Andrew Gibb, volume associate editor, is the area head of history, theory, and criticism in the School of Theatre and Dance at Texas Tech University. He has published work in *Theatre Symposium, Theatre History Studies*, the *Latin American Theatre Review*, and the *Texas Theatre* on Chicano Literature.

Kyla Kazuschyk has created costumes for the Santa Fe Opera, the Washington National Opera, the Florida Grand Opera, the Colorado Shakespeare Festival, and the Texas Shakespeare Festival. Professional design credits include *The Book Club Play* and *Disgraced*, both for Louisiana's Swine Palace Theatre, and *Savage/Love*, a work of physical theatre performed at the 2016 Edinburgh Fringe Festival. She currently teaches, manages the costume shop, and designs costumes at Louisiana State University. Kyla enjoys creating costumes for competitive dance troupes as well as uniforms for the dance teams of the National Basketball Association's Orlando Magic and Detroit Pistons.

Leah Lowe is an associate professor in Departments of Theatre and American Studies at Vanderbilt University. Her artistic background is in directing. She directs plays at Vanderbilt and around Nashville. Her scholarly interests are focused on American theatre audiences of the late nineteenth century. She earned her MFA in directing from the University of Minnesota and her PhD from Florida State University.

Michele Majer, keynote speaker, is an assistant professor at Bard Graduate Center, specializing in the history of clothing and textiles from the eighteenth through the twentieth century. She is also a research associate at the Cora Ginsburg Gallery in New York, dealing in antique clothing and textiles. She is the editor of and a contributor to *Staging Fashion, 1880–1920: Jane Hading, Lily Elsie, Billie Burke* (2012), and she has contributed articles, reviews, and essays to publications such as *The Age of Napoleon: Costume from Revolution and Empire; Romance and Chivalry: History and Literature Reflected in Nineteenth-Century French Painting; Studies in the Decorative Arts; Design and Culture*, as well as the annual Cora Ginsburg catalogue. She has also lectured widely and presented conference papers in the United States and the United Kingdom.

Sarah McCarroll, volume editor, is an associate professor of theatre at Georgia Southern University, where she is also the resident costume designer and costume shop manager for the Theatre and Performance program. Sarah's research interests include period dress and movement, the historical body, and British theatre of the late nineteenth century. Her work has appeared in *Theatre Symposium* and in the anthology *Theatre, Performance and Cognition: Languages, Bodies and Ecologies*. Sarah's PhD is from Indiana University and her MFA is from the University of Alabama.

Caitlin Quinn is the Assistant Professor of Costume Design at the University of South Dakota. In addition to her teaching and design work there, she has designed costumes for Stay Awake Theatre in New York; The Organic Theatre Company in Illinois; Black Hills Playhouse in South Dakota; Wake Forest University in North Carolina; Saint Mary's University in Minnesota; and others. Her research interests include rendering techniques for costume designers, modern style tribes, and social signifiers in costume design. Her teaching interests include costume design, costume history, costume crafts, and rendering for costume designers.

Jorge Sandoval is a member of the Faculty of Fine Arts at the University of Lethbridge in Lethbridge, Canada, and a PhD candidate in the Department of Film, Television, and Scenography at Aalto University, in Helsinki, Finland. He holds an MFA in Theatre and Interdisciplinary Studies from the University of Regina and a BFA in Art History and Studio Art from Concordia University in Montreal. He actively researches and works with issues related to queer identity, theatre and performance, and the production of space. His most recent artistic work includes the curation and presentation of artwork at the exhibition "Mapping the Body" at the Penny Art Gallery of the University of Lethbridge in March 2017, and the performance of his work "Wearing the Other" at the Men in Dance Festival in Regina, Saskatchewan, in January 2016.

David S. Thompson is the Annie Louise Harrison Waterman Professor of Theatre at Agnes Scott College, where he has also served as Chair of the Department of Theatre and Dance. He is a past president of the Southeastern Theatre Conference, the sponsoring entity for *Theatre Symposium*, and frequent contributor to the organization's publications. In addition, he was the 2014 recipient of the Suzanne M. Davis Memorial Award for distinguished service to the theatre.